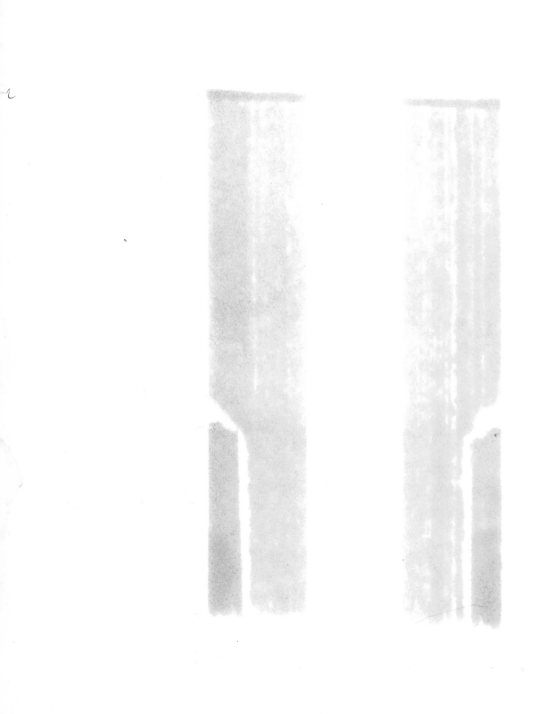

ILLUSTRATED MYTHS
OF NATIVE AMERICA

The Northeast, Southeast, Great Lakes and Great Plains

TIM McNEESE

Illustrated by
RICHARD HOOK

BLANDFORD

A BLANDFORD BOOK

First published in the UK 1998 by Blandford
a Cassell imprint

Cassell plc
Wellington House
125 Strand
London WC2R 0BB

Copyright © 1998 Cassell plc
Text copyright © 1998 Tim McNeese

The right of Tim McNeese to be identified as the author and of Richard Hook as
the illustrator of this work has been asserted by them under the provisions of
the UK Copyright, Designs and Patents Act 1988.

Distributed in the United States by Sterling Publishing Co., Inc.
387 Park Avenue South, New York, NY 10016–8810

A Cataloguing-in-Publication Data entry for this title is available from the
British Library

ISBN 0–7137–2666–0

Designed by Chris Bell
Printed by Kyodo Printing Co., Singapore

CONTENTS

INTRODUCTION

IN THE DAYS BEFORE the arrival and permanent settlement of Europeans in the early sixteenth century, the land that today comprises the continental United States was a vast wilderness, a place abundant with wildlife, where rivers carved their courses throughout its many ridges and mountains, verdant valleys and barren plains. This primeval region was the home of the earliest human inhabitants of North America.

When the European explorers arrived, the land was occupied by a patchwork quilt of varied tribal groups, each with its own unique arts, customs and social practices. These groups spoke many different languages, and communication between tribes was often difficult. This, together with a host of other factors, including the geography of where each tribe lived, caused these Native Americans to develop individual lifestyles.

This book presents a slice of the mythology and legends of four regional groups of Native Americans: the Northeastern, the Southeastern, the Great Lakes and Ohio Valley, and the Great Plains culture groups. The first two dominated the Eastern Woodland area of the modern-day United States before the coming of the Europeans. The tribes of the Northeast ranged throughout the region from Maine to the Great Lakes, stretching south to the Commonwealth of Virginia. Many of them hugged the Atlantic seaboard, extending their unique cultural influences from Massachusetts Bay to the tidewaters of the Chesapeake. The peoples of the Southeast included the mound-building tribes of the pre-Columbian Adena, Hopewell and Mississippian eras. They were scattered from the banks of the lower Mississippi River across the modern Gulf and Appalachian Mountain states of Tennessee, the Carolinas, Mississippi, Alabama and Georgia. These two regionally based, tribal–cultural groups shared common practices of daily life, from hunting to domestic agriculture. Yet each left its own mark on the land and on the history of the early occupation of North America.

Located along the banks of the Great Lakes and among the many rivers of the Ohio River valley, other tribes – many of them Algonquian in language stock – occupied the land, serving as rivals and enemies of the Iroquois of the Northeast. These tribes practised hunting, fishing and domesticated agriculture, and roamed about in birch-bark canoes. The region in which they lived included the modern-day states of Minnesota, Wisconsin, Michigan, Ohio, Indiana and Illinois.

Out on the boundless and nearly treeless prairies lived the cultural group known as the Great Plains tribes. These Native Americans spread their influence from the sage-brush lands of western Texas to the north as far as Canada. Tribes such as the Sioux, Cheyenne, Blackfoot and Pawnee dominated the region and, by the middle of the eighteenth century, had created a lifestyle that depended on the horse for transportation and the success of the buffalo hunt as the basis of its economy.

For hundreds of years, these culture groups developed an elaborate oral tradition of legends, tales and myths concerning their ancestors, their gods, their tribe and the world of nature that surrounded them. These stories were passed from generation to generation, and many were not recorded in any permanent form until the eighteenth, nineteenth and even twentieth centuries. Much of this effort to preserve the oral heritage of Native Americans has been a co-operative one between Native American speakers and a host of ethnologists, linguists, dialecticians, army officers, explorers and anthropologists. Now this 'literature' of America's first people has been preserved for all time. In this volume there are sixty or so such stories, meant not only to entertain the reader but also to enlighten – to present the Native American and his world – for much of that world did not survive the arrival of the Europeans to the New World. Here a remnant of that world remains, one that will, I trust, never be destroyed.

NOTE TO THE READER

THE STORIES INCLUDED in this book reveal both the differences and also the similarities between the tribes of North America. While it is impossible to categorize all these legends into convenient pigeonholes of theme and subject, many reveal several key motifs.

In some of these tales, the protagonist, nearly always a male member of a tribe or a male animal, is involved in an adventure or experience that the narrator wishes his or her audience to apply to their lives or from which they can extract a message or certain information. Common motifs include visitations to supernatural lands, especially to the sky or stars; transformation experiences, wherein the protagonist becomes something new, such as a tree, a star or an animal; a contest, race or duel with an object at stake that is highly prized by the participants, such as immortality, beauty, great power or the maiden daughter of a great chief; dreams or visions that the protagonist experiences a visitation or portent of some future event to come; 'numbskull' tales with half-witted characters who must laugh at their own stupidity or naïvety; taboo legends, featuring a character who decides to throw caution to the wind and do something that is forbidden or warned against; and tales of endless supplies of food, inspired by Native Americans whose diets were not always balanced and who experienced, from time to time, true hunger and near starvation.

◆

References in source citations to *JAFL* refer to the *Journal of American Folklore*, *BAE* to the *Bureau of American Ethnology* and *BAEAR* to *Bureau of American Ethnology Annual Report*.

PART 1
THE NORTHEAST

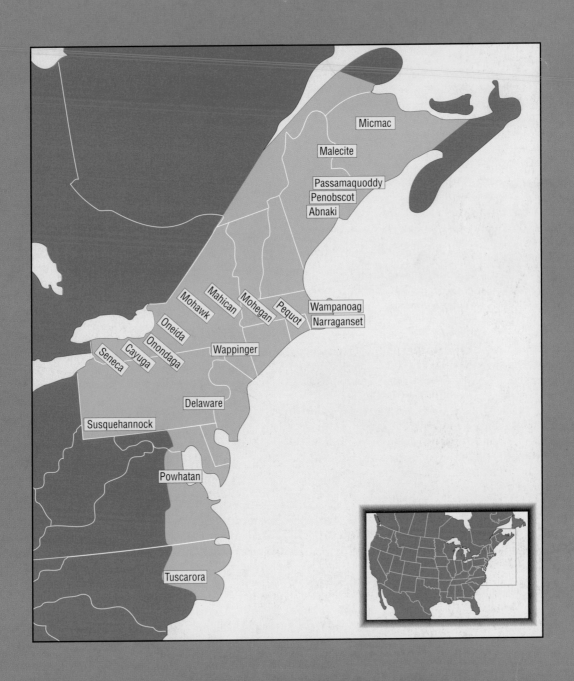

Micmac

Malecite

Passamaquoddy
Penobscot
Abnaki

Mahican

Mohawk

Mohegan

Pequot

Wampanoag
Narraganset

Oneida

Onondaga

Wappinger

Seneca

Cayuga

Delaware

Susquehannock

Powhatan

Tuscarora

TRIBES OF THE NORTHEAST

Although modern anthropologists continue to push back the earliest accepted date for Native American occupation of the great woodlands east of the Mississippi, a comfortable period lies somewhere between 5,000 and 7,000 years ago. In western New York a social order of natives arose called the Lamoka Culture. These ancient peoples utilized projectile points that have since been uncovered in other locales, including eastern Michigan, the Ohio valley and points east to the Atlantic coast. Their tools and weapons included bone and antler knives, fishing hooks, awls, hide scrapers and even whistles. Not only did they knap projectile points, they also busied themselves with polishing stones, including pestles and mortars.

To the east a neighbouring culture, the Laurentian Culture, developed at the same time and was longer lasting. Centred in eastern New York and extending east to New England and north to the St Lawrence River, this culture carved, beyond the usual kitchen tools, harpoons and slate spear points.

Such stone-based culture groups would over time give way to the Old Copper Culture, which peaked between 4,000 and 3,000 years ago and lasted for a couple of millennia. Centred on the Great Lakes, this hunting and fishing culture introduced an extensive use of metals. With copper ore in abundance in the region, the natives began to create from solid copper practical items for daily use, including knives, chisels, spear points and axes. Such metal items spread quickly throughout the eastern woodlands as they became prized trade goods. With these metal implements, the Native Americans were able to make dug-out canoes. Other sorts of canoes, as well as a variety of different items, were made from birch bark. These people also began to develop forms of clay pottery.

Early Woodland Stage

Around 3,000 years ago, and lasting until about 500 years before Christ, another phase in the advancement of the prehistoric tribes of the Northeast developed: the Early Woodland Stage. At this time the Indians were noted for the building of earthen mounds. Among the most important mound-building cultures was the Adena (see page 84) which developed a highly centralized social structure and served as a culture of origin for Indian splinter groups that migrated over time to the east, as far as the Chesapeake region, and further north into modern-day New York state and New England. Such mound-building activities were possible only where tribes led a less nomadic, more sedentary life, and this was possible only when sustained farming could be practised.

This culture group became increasingly dependent on a permanent agricultural system. Certainly, hunting, fishing and the harvesting of coastal shellfish remained mainstays, even as agriculture made powerful inroads into their native diets. Vegetables common today, such as squash, were finding their way into the fare of these Northeastern tribes. They were also growing gourds, sunflowers and marsh elder. Over time these plants and vegetables provided between a third and nearly half of the daily food supply of many Northeastern tribes.

This new level of agricultural dependence speeded up the growth of native populations simultaneously in the Northeastern region and in other parts of North America. With this sedentary lifestyle, tribes could develop more complex social, political and economic systems, bringing a new level of sophistication and a higher standard of living to the tribes of the region.

Hopewellian Culture

This Early Woodland Stage of progress eventually gave way to another phase, which is known by anthropologists as the Middle Woodland Stage. Beginning about 100 BC and lasting until about AD 500–700, this phase witnessed the coming of the Hopewellian era. Still a mound-oriented culture, these tribes began planting and harvesting new crops that had made their way up from Central America and Mexico. Hopewellian mound sites have yielded for the modern anthropologist and archaeologist a great collection of artefacts that help to explain the lifestyles of such Native Americans. Copper tools were common among the Hopewell peoples. Other artefacts include wooden and stone tools and weapons, obsidian objects, carved stone pipes and statues. In a grave of one Hopewell mound, archaeologists unearthed a cache of 60,000 pearls.

These Hopewellian people were extraordinarily domesticated. Corn, beans and tobacco were soon added to their farming efforts. Northeastern tribes in this era began building huts called wigwams – oval structures with curved, dome-like roofs. Tree saplings provided the framework for such houses, which were covered with large sections of bark or with animal skins. Trade flourished among the tribes. Tools were made out of copper, bone, antler and stone. Women created elaborate clay pottery. Northeastern Indian art included decorations on pottery and various forms of carving, including tobacco pipes whose bowls represented forest animals and human heads. The musical instruments produced included woodwinds, such as panpipes, and many varieties of drum and rattle.

It is not known why the Hopewellian Culture died out. Mound-building faded from the scene in the Northeastern region, although it continued to be prominent in the American Southeast, from the Mississippi River valley across to the coastal areas of modern-day South Carolina, Georgia and Florida.

In the Northeast, throughout the period from 1000 until the arrival of the Europeans in the sixteenth and seventeenth centuries, the culture became less monolithic, as various tribal identities developed, many of which were intact by the time of the European contact. Agriculture continued to dominate in the region, populations rose in number, the number and size of Northeastern settlements increased and their cultures became more inventive and creative. All across the north, from the Great Lakes to modern-day New York and New England, through to the maritime provinces of modern-day Canada, tribal distinctions and familial clans developed. Languages such as the Algonquian, Iroquoian and Siouan took on their distinctive elements.

Indeed, the heyday of early, pre-Columbian tribal groups occurred in the years following 1250. During these centuries, the Eastern tribes continued to progress, advancing their political, economic and social structures, as well as their individual technologies, which gradually produced better weapons, tools, housing and means of transportation. By 1500, the intricate tribal structures founded across North America and particularly in the regions east of the Mississippi, as well as the American Southwest, were being deeply influenced or even destroyed with the coming of the Europeans.

Native Cultures of the Northeast

When English religious refugees landed in 1621 at Cape Cod in modern-day Massachusetts, they discovered a group of Native Americans unique to a place and time. The Eastern Woodland tribes had already spread throughout the region stretching from the Atlantic seaboard to the Mississippi River in the west. One contemporary account, typical in its descriptiveness of a small party of local natives, Wampanoags, who were led by the famous Massasoit, a noted sachem (chief) to the tribe, reads as follows:

> On this day came again the savage, and brought with him five other proper men. They had every man a deer's skin on him and the principal of them had a wild-cat's skin, or such like, on the one arm. They had most of them long hose up to their groins, close made, and above their groins to their waist another leather. They were altogether like the Irish trousers . . . On their heads long hair to the shoulders, only cut before,

some trussed up before with a feather, broad wise, like a fan, another a fox tail hanging out. They were in their faces in part or in whole painted, some black, some red, some yellow, and some white, some with crosses, and other fanciful works. Some had skins on them and some naked, all strong, tall men in appearance.

Such encounters were a continuation of the process of early colonial contact between native populations and the Europeans, first brought on by visiting explorers such as Hudson, Verrazano and LaSalle, and by later arrivals such as the Pilgrim Fathers, who planted themselves along the Massachusetts coast and remained.

The native cultures that these early whites encountered were nothing like anything they had seen in the Old World. Though there were always tribal variations from one regional group to another, many of these native tribes had much in common with each other. In the North-east, the Woodland tribes, as described by the eyewitness account just quoted, wore a variety of distinct costumes. The men wore breechclouts in the summer, donning leggings and shirts of deer skin during the winter. Women wore deer-skin dresses and leggings, and everyone wore moccasins. Footwear designs varied from tribe to tribe, with most winter models being lined with rabbit fur. Some Atlantic coastal tribes wore grass and hemp skirts and robes adorned with wild turkey feathers sewn into the material.

For the most part, the tribes that comprise the Eastern Woodland ethnic groups may be divided into two language stocks: the Algonquian and Iroquoian. While some Algonquian tribes ranged to the west, as far as the region of the Great Lakes, several located themselves in the New England area. North of Maine were the Micmac peoples with their traditional lands encompassing the Canadian maritime provinces of Nova Scotia, Cape Breton Island and New Brunswick. Other Algonquian tribes included the Passamaquoddy and Penobscot tribes, which shared territory in Maine. These two, along with the Malecites and a few other, smaller tribes, are sometimes referred to as the Abenakis.

Early European contact with the Penobscot tribe resulted in a belief that this tribe was the centre of a great American kingdom. Later sixteenth- and early seventeenth-century New World maps began including a lavish city situated along the Norumbega River (the Penobscot River). According to the stories, the Penobscots were ruled by a great king named Bashaba, whose lands stretched to the south as far as Virginia. Subsequent explorations revealed that the Penobscots' village was a small one and their chief was in fact no king at all.

A smaller tribe in the New England area was the Wampanoags, whose history is inter-twined with the Plymouth Pilgrims and the founding of the Massachusetts Bay Colony. The tribe known as the 'People of the Small Bay', the Narragansett, lived in Rhode Island. Neighbouring Connecticut (derived from the Indian word Quonoktacut, which translates as 'River Whose Water is Driven by Tides') was the homeland of the Mohegans, the Pequots and Wappinger tribes.

Modern-day New York, with its many rivers, lakes and ranging mountains, was the home of a variety of significant Indian groups, some Algonquin, others Iroquois. The Mahicans, who are sometimes confused with the Connecti-cut Mohegans, lived along the upper Hudson River country. Further to the south were the Delawares, who were known among themselves as the Lenni Lenape (which translates as ' Original People'). The use of such references made by certain tribes concerning themselves and their beginnings are common in Native American stories. Many tribes told creation myths and, in the process, explained how human life began not only on earth but also among their specific tribe or people.

The Iroquois

When Algonquian tribes spoke of their neigh-bours the Haudenosaunee, they referred to them as the Iroquois, a word that means 'terrible people' or 'frightening people'. In time, the Hau-denosaunee adopted the name for themselves. The Iroquoian language stock was shared by numerous tribes. In more modern times, when the term Iroquois is used, it applies to the five tribes who lived along the Mohawk River in cen-tral New York. These tribes came to unify themselves into a democratic confederacy known as the Five Nations. The original tribes of the Five Nations were the Senecas, Cayuga, Onondaga, Oneida and Mohawks. (Neighbouring Narragansetts gave the Mohawks their name, which means 'man-eaters', since the Mohawks had a reputation for occasional cannibalism.) In the early years of the eighteenth century, a sixth nation was added when the Tuscarora tribe was adopted into the confederacy after it had been driven from its North Carolina homelands by intruding Europeans and Anglo-Americans. The Tuscarora migrated north, joining up with the Oneida. They were officially accepted into the confederacy in 1715. Other Iroquoian tribes located in the Northeast included the Susquehanna, who ranged in southeastern Pennsylvania and the northern Maryland region, in the vicinity of the river that bears their name and flows into Chesapeake Bay.

The advent of the Five Nations confederacy came soon after the arrival of the first Europeans along the Atlantic in the later sixteenth century. Legend relates the coming of an Indian prophet named Dekanawida, who brought to the Iroquois a vision of a 'Great Peace'. This prophecy foresaw the confederacy, in which the tribes of the Iroquois would live together, united against common foes. A Mohawk chief named Hiawatha founded the Five Nations confederacy around 1570. He visited many Iroquois villages, preaching unity and condemning the practice of cannibalism. Hiawatha's message was not without its critics, most notably an Onondaga chief named Todadaho. According to legend, Hiawatha had to agree to an intertribal council which featured more Onondaga representatives than the other tribes were allowed. In addition, the Onondaga village was the first meeting site of the Five Nations. (Some Iroquois legends concerning Hiawatha portray Todadaho as a Medusa-like monster with snakes pouring out of his head which Hiawatha combs out.) Under the political arrangements inherent in the Five Nations agreement, member tribes retained their independence in self-governance, with the league having jurisdiction only in cases of inter-tribal concern.

Confederacies among Eastern Woodland tribes were not confined solely to the Iroquois confederacy of the Five Nations. Historically, various confederacies were formed periodically for purposes of defence. Some Algonquian tribes formed confederacies, the most notable among them being the Delaware Confederacy. Others included the Wabanaki Confederacy, which saw the unification of the Malecites, Micmacs, Penobscots, Passamaquoddys and others, and the Wappinger Confederacy, which brought together several smaller tribes in Connecticut and across the East River to Manhattan Island, where one member tribe, the Manhattans, sold the island to Dutch settlers for the oft-quoted bargain-basement price of twenty-four dollars. Yet the confederacy of the Five Nations was the most complicated union of related tribes, encompassing complex political and military concerns.

Iroquoian Intertribal Structures

Iroquois tribes established their social and familial structures around clans, each of which had an animal as its representative. Several interrelated families formed the basis of a clan. Members of the clan could claim common ancestors. Clan membership was always traced through the women of each family, thus making for a matrilineal society. In practical terms, this meant that a child born into his mother's Turtle clan, for example, would, after marrying, have children who were members of his wife's clan. The two original Iroquois clans were the Deer and the Wolf. Offshoots of the Deer would later include the Hawk, Heron and Snipe clans, while the Wolf clan produced the clans of the Deer, the Turtle and the Beaver. Intermarriage between members of the original Deer and Wolf clans was forbidden, which helped the tribes keep blood relatives from taking each other as husband and wife.

The Iroquois Long House

The Iroquois lived in fortified villages, surrounded by palisades and consisting of several 'long houses'. These bark-covered dwellings, known to the Iroquois as *ganonh'sees*, were built by the men of the tribe and owned by the women. They provided accommodation for anywhere from five to twenty families. On average, they were about sixty feet (eighteen metres) long with a width of eighteen to twenty feet (five to seven metres). The roof was often sloped or took on the shape of a barrel arch, with a line of ridge poles running the length of the house. The building's ridge peak was high, rising twenty feet (seven metres) from the earthen floor. The walls of the long house were a latticed frame-work covered with wide strips of birch bark measuring approximately four by six feet (one by two metres). In regions where birch was scarce, the Iroquois relied on elm, ash, cedar, basswood or hemlock. The walls of the long house were windowless, with doors at both ends. Such an arrangement proved cool and airy in the summer and snug in the winter. Inside, each family hung skins up for curtains, providing at least rudimentary privacy.

The Algonquian Wigwam

In contrast to the Iroquois multi-family dwellings, the Algonquins more often relied on the construction of wigwams, which tended to house fewer people and thus fewer families. Much smaller than the long houses of their neighbours, they were designed as bark-covered domes with the centre rising to a height slightly taller than an adult male standing erect. The outer dimensions of many Algonquian wigwams measured fourteen by twenty feet (four by seven metres). A fire burned constantly inside, at the wigwam's centre, with an opening for smoke at the top of the wigwam. Along the outer wall, away from the central fire, the Algonquins slept on woven mats. Dried food and baskets hung from the support poles. While Iroquois men built their long houses, Algonquian women built their wigwams, just as many Plains women were responsible for the construction of their tepees (see page 125).

Food Sources of the Woodland Tribes

The diet of the peoples of the Eastern Woodland area was a varied one, supplied through agricultural endeavours, gathering, fishing and hunting. A strict delineation of sexual roles was practised: gathering and the raising of crops were considered women's work, while catching fish, harvesting shellfish and hunting fell into the male domain.

The forested lands of the Northeastern region were teeming with wild game, creating a hunter's paradise prior to the arrival of the Europeans. The Algonquins hunted deer, caribou, moose, elk and bear, supplementing their diet with gathering and fishing. They also hunted smaller game, such as racoons, muskrats, porcupines, woodchucks and beaver, as well as a bevy of gamebirds including ducks, geese and grouse. Farming was difficult in the northern reaches because of the short growing season.

The Iroquois, located generally south of the Algonquins, relied on hunting and agriculture, raising a variety of crops including beans, squash and maize (the crops referred to as the 'Three Sisters'). As limited as this selection of crops sounds, the Indians in fact raised many kinds of corn (including a popping variety, which, when mixed with maple syrup, created a sweet delicacy that more modern Americans refer to as 'Cracker Jacks'), plus at least sixty types of bean and eight different varieties of squash. Add to their culinary repertoire such foods as potatoes, pumpkins and a plethora of berries, including strawberries, cranberries and blackberries, and throw in such exotic items as sunflowers, mushrooms and a variety of nuts, and you have the makings of a true tribal feast. Blander foods were often made more flavoursome by using natural seasonings, including wild onions and wild ginger. Salt was seldom used if at all; for the Onondaga to season their foods with salt was considered taboo.

In addition to a wide variety of foods, the Northeastern tribes had many different drinks on tap. The Iroquois, for example, had at least a dozen, including 'corn coffee' and teas made by boiling roots such as sassafras. Berries were squeezed and boiled into juicy libations. Some tribes cooked up a brew that tasted much like lemonade by harvesting the berries found on the staghorn sumac plant.

Hunting was more than a source of food; the hides of each hunter's catch were generally worked into clothing and furry sleeping covers. Typically, the men of the Northeastern Woodland tribes fished in the spring and summer, leaving the autumn season for their extensive hunting expeditions. (Winter was a sedentary season for nearly all the Northeastern tribes.) The chief weapon used by the Northeastern tribes in their hunting was the bow and arrow.

While hunting and fishing provided meat for the stewpots of both the Iroquois and the Algonquins, the women of many tribes practised a crude agriculture. The chief crop was corn. Nearly every tribe that grew corn had a story concerning this chief crop's origins. The Chippewa told a story of a stranger named Mon-daw-min who wrestled with a Chippewa hunter. When the hunter defeated his opponent, on the spot where Mon-daw-min died, there the first corn grew. (The legend is ironic, considering that the Chippewa did not traditionally grow corn!) Corn-growing became such an important source of food for the Iroquois that the word they used to describe it translates as 'our life'. Women and those children of the tribe old enough to work in the fields raised the maize. In preparation for their agricultural pursuits, the Northeastern tribes would notch a ring around the base of each tree that needed clearing, a practice known to the Europeans who later followed this method, which they referred to as 'girdling'. With a lack of fertilizers, these tribal agronomists planted crops in their fields for approximately twenty growing seasons and then, as the soil was sapped of its nutrients, cleared more land and began growing their crops once more on virgin land.

Nearly every activity of the Eastern Woodland Indians was connected to some manifestation of the spirit world, including and especially corn production. Native tribes marked the planting, growing, cultivation and harvesting stages of corn with a festival. In fact, festivals marked the harvests of all crops.

Once harvested, these crops were often dried to preserve them. The Iroquois built wooden cribs where they stored their corn. Women also ground corn into meal, which would generally have a longer shelf life. Squash and pumpkins had their outer shells removed, and the edible portions were cut into long spirals and hung on pegs and sinew lines to dry. The Iroquois dug storage pits, lined them with bark pieces and filled them with beans or meat or dried fruits, covering each pit with a slab of thick bark.

Eastern Woodlands Religion and Mythology

For all native cultures found in North America, religion played a dominant role in the day-to-day activities of each tribe and of its individual members. The Eastern Woodland tribes were no exception. Their religion was generally an extremely personal one, practical in nature, and having to do with an individual's daily needs. However, native religion is crowded with a pantheon of deities, both good and evil, and stratified hierarchies of various gods and goddesses. Superstition marked the perimeters of their religion and defined the rituals, festivals, dances and belief systems.

Like the ancient Greeks, Native Americans faced the daily potential of offending the supernatural forces who controlled their naturalistic lives. Appeasement to such dieties in the form of gifts and offerings was common. Failure to appeal to the appropriate supernatural being might bring drought, sickness, war or something as basic as a harsh northern wind.

Both the Iroquois and the Algonquins recognized an all-pervasive deity, a spirit that permeated the entire scope of the natural world around them. Though similar in nature, each greater tribal group gave their all-knowing deity a different name. The Iroquois called their great spirit Orenda; the Algonquins referred to theirs as Manitou. Their destinies depended on the responses of their greatest deity. However, unlike the Christian God, which many white missionaries likened to the natives' Orenda or Manitou, these supernatural beings were actually the embodiment of many spirits that lived and occupied all the objects common to each Indian's existence. Such a theology gave definition to Northeastern Indians' views of their own afterlife. Natives believed that their life after death would exist as a mirror image of their earthly lives, in much the same way as ancient Egyptians imagined theirs. Once one died, it was believed, life would continue in a spirit world where human needs such as eating and sleeping would continue. No Northeastern tribes believed in any sort of punishment in connection with their concept of the afterlife. The Iroquois, for example, had a belief in an underworld, but it was not the Hades of the Greeks; rather, it was a lovely ground where disease was non-existent and war was no longer waged. This underworld, it was believed, was where their ancestors resided, a place ruled by a being known as the Mother of Animals.

The Iroquois also wove intricate and elaborate stories and myths into their religious framework, involving gods who took the form of various animals, which, on occasion, took human form. This idea led to the concept of animal-based clans such as the Deer, Wolf, Turtle and so on. Supreme among Iroquois gods was the thunder god, named Hinu. He was an even-handed god, kind to those who were deserving and a punisher of evil. The Iroquois courted Hinu's favour by burning tobacco in ceremonial rituals. (Incidentally, Hinu also provided the Iroquois people with an explanation of how the dinosaurs, whose gigantic bones native Americans occasionally discovered, disappeared from the earth. He had destroyed them long ago, since they would have proved a constant menace and danger to man.) Hinu makes an appearance in a variety of Iroquois myths, including some that have him residing behind Niagara Falls (Ne-ah-ga-rah to the Iroquois) and rescuing a young Indian girl from going over the Falls in her canoe (she later became the Maiden of the Mist).

Helping fill the ranks of the Iroquois dieties were Ka-tash-huaht, the North Wind, who brought cold and death to the tribes; Goweh, the war god, to whom only Iroquois could pray; Tarhuhyiawahku, the Holder of the Heavens, who created the Six Nations of the Iroquois; and a host of others, including the good and evil twins Tsentsa and Taweskare, sons of the West Wind (Hinu's brother), who created the earth, and the Three Sisters, the trio of spirits who watched over the harvests of corn, beans and squash.

In addition, the Iroquois envisioned stories and myths that were sometimes crowded with lesser supernatural creatures, including wizards, pygmies, witches, giants made of stone and weird creatures called Great Heads, which were little more than gigantic heads with a pair of legs in lieu of a neck to give them a threatening mobility. Despite modern expectations, pygmies

were not creatures to be taken lightly. They had special powers to create massive rock formations, could turn stones into any shape of their choosing and were able to kill monsters infinitely larger than they, even giants. Such elfish creatures, as revealed in the myths, were always giving their assistance to hapless natives through their life's course.

The Algonquian concept of spirit power was, as we have already noted, embodied in the being they called Manitou, who, like the Iroquois Orenda, was understood to be multiple spirits, literally thousands in number, who in combination created a supernatural essence that permeated all things in nature. Thus their concept of Manitou was of many 'Manitous', each wielding its own level of power and potency. The highest power of Manitou was, for some tribes, called Kitshi Manitou, meaning chief in the Algonquian language. Other tribes, such as the Abenaki, believed in the existence of Kechi Niwaski, a god of good and giver of life. Tribal myths describe Kechi Niwaski as having created the first Abenaki from stone. Unhappy with their appearance, Kechi Niwaski carved another pair, male and female, from wood, then gave them life as flesh-and-blood humans.

Most noted among all Algonquian Manitous was a spirit known as Manabozho, which translates variously as 'God of Light', 'Ruler of the Sun' and 'Great White Hare'. Commonly, Menabozho gave the sun power to make its daily course through the heavens. This god was capable of changing his shape, sometimes taking the form of a human and walking on earth. Some Algonquian tribes heralded the first arrivals of Europeans to their waters as the arrival of Manabozho as a man.

As in Iroquois mythology, Algonquian deities include good and evil twins, Malsum and Glooscap, who are similar to Tsentsa and Taweskare. In cause of their rivalries, Glooscap kills Malsum (or Malsumis), the maker of evil. In an underground world of magic, Malsum then takes on life as an evil wolf. There are many stories about Glooscap's adventures, and they often culminate in his leaving earth in a birch-bark canoe, paddling towards the heavens. Some tales end with the Algonquin anticipating the future second coming of Glooscap.

Additional supernatural and magical creatures may be found in Algonquian mythology in which ghosts eat humans, witches cast spells and sorcerers practise their arts with great powers at hand. As with many Native American tribes, the Algonquins believed in out-of-body experiences, which would allow a human being's body and spirit to separate, allowing spiritual adventures in other physical forms, as in the taking on of an animal's body. A designated caste of priests called shamans claimed to have the power to send their spirits, upon falling into a trance, on visitations to animals, or to the spirit world, where they might commune with an ancient ancestor or a recently departed soul. One caution an Algonquian magic man's visiting spirit had to remember was not to take food or drink from another spirit, as this action would forever separate the spirit from its physical body, which, once spiritless, would die.

Prophets, Magicians and Shamans

While shamans wielded great spiritual power as tribal holy men, other men filled additional roles as prophets, magicians and great healers known as herbalists. Algonquian magicians or sorcerers claimed power over some aspects of the physical world, including the ability to halt the coming of natural disasters. Such men performed incantations and rituals which called forth supernatural entities from the underworld. Sometimes their ceremonies involved wild, gyrating dances. They claimed the ability to remove evil spirits from a possessed member of their tribe.

Algonquins sought the services of not only magicians but tribal doctors as well. Herbalists sometimes practised their tribal medicine as individuals, while others became members of a medical society. These practitioners of the healing arts had a great working knowledge of the natural medicinal properties of a wide variety of locally grown plants and used them in potions and as curative powders and other medicines.

False Face Societies

Similar healers could be found among the Iroquois as well. Some of their medicine men formed a special group called the False Face Society, whose purpose was not only to heal the diseased but to keep them from getting sick in the first place. To do this, they carved wooden masks which bore hideous and contorted facial features designed to protect the tribe by scaring off the evil spirits that carried disease. While each mask was handmade and no two were ever exactly alike, there were about a dozen basic false-face designs. Some featured twisted mouth formations, others had protruding tongues and still others had thick lips and mocking looks. To gain membership of the False Face Society, it was necessary only to dream that you were a member. After such a dream, the candidate hosted a banquet and was accepted into the society. All members of the False Face Society were male, with only one exception. A women served as the Keeper of the False Faces. Her role was particularly significant since she was the only one of the tribe who knew the identities of each member of the False Face Society.

In action, members of the False Face Society would enter the lodge of a sick person and carry out a series of incantations, dancing around the victim, shaking turtle-shell rattles and sprinkling ashes all about the place. To ward off disease in general from their villages, False Face Society members performed additional incantations, generally each spring and autumn, designed to scare away the evil spirits intent on doing physical harm to unwary villagers.

Other tribes also wore masks, but not necessarily for the same reasons as the Iroquois False Face Society. The Delaware tribe, for example, used masks in their corn rituals and ceremonies. (Such masks were also worn by the Iroquois members of the Huskface Society, who made their face covering out of cornhusks rather than wood.) Algonquin corn masks were always prevalent at the annual Corn Harvest Dance, as a tribute to the Mother Corn deity.

MYTHS AND LEGENDS
OF THE NORTHEAST

THE FIRST PEOPLE AND THE FIRST CORN

Penobscot and Passamaquoddy

A LONG TIME AGO, Klos-kur-beh, the Great Teacher, lived all alone. He was visited one day by a man who claimed to be his nephew. He stood before Klos-kur-beh saying, 'The foam of the waters bore me as a child. The winds blew about and caused the waves of the sea to foam. The sun warmed the sea foam and the warmth produced life. I am that life. I am a healthy and young being, and I have come to live with you and give you aid in all the things that you do.'

At noon on another day, Klos-kur-beh was visited by a young maiden. She stood before the Great Teacher and the youthful man and called them both 'her offspring'. She spoke on: 'I have come to live with you, my children. I bring love with me which I will give to you. I am also strong, and I have the power to grant this gift. If you give me love and give me my heart's desire, all the world will love me, including the animals. You may find comfort in me for I am young and strong. I was born out of a beautiful plant. The dew fell on a leaf, warmed by the sun. Its warmth produced life and I am that life.'

Klos-kur-beh prayed a song of praise to the Great Spirit for the arrival of the young man and the maiden. Soon afterwards, the two became husband and wife and she produced the first children in the world. She was the first mother. Klos-kur-beh taught the two many things about life and performed mighty works in their presence. When he determined that his work with them was completed, he left them and travelled in the Northland, waiting for the day when he felt it was time to return to them.

The numbers of people continued to multiply and increase. A famine fell upon the people and the First Mother became increasingly sorrowful. She began to distance herself from her husband and stayed away from him from morning until the evening cast long shadows. Since he loved her very much, her husband was saddened to watch First Mother grieve.

One day he followed after his wife when she left him that morning. He trailed her to the ford of a river and waited along its bank for her to return. When she returned later in the day, she began to sing for joy as she crossed the river. It seemed that she was happy as long as her feet remained in the water. When she emerged on the opposite bank, her husband noticed a long green blade behind her right foot. She stooped down and pulled the blade out, throwing it aside. Then she began to sadden once again.

When the husband followed her to their home, he encouraged her to come outside and look at the beauty of the setting sun. As they watched the sun, their

Source

Natalie Curtis
Burlin, *The
Indians' Book*,
New York:
Harper and
Brothers, 1907,
pp. 3–6

seven children joined them, crying to their mother, 'We are hungry, mother, and it will soon be nightfall. Will you bring us some food?' The First Mother began to cry and reassured them that they would have plenty to eat in seven moons. Her husband did not understand what she meant nor what he could possibly do to make his beautiful wife happy again. 'There is nothing you can do to make me happy,' she said to him.

Desperate for answers, the husband left home and travelled to the Northland, where he took counsel with the Great Teacher, his old mentor. After receiving counsel for seven suns, the husband returned to his wife, prepared to do for her whatever she asked of him. This pleased the First Mother and she gave him the following instructions: 'First, you must kill me, then allow two men to drag my body all over a field, all the time dragging me by my hair. In the middle of the field, they must bury my bones. After the passing of seven moons, they must return to the field and collect all they find there rising from the soil. They must eat what they find, for it is my flesh. Do not eat my bones, but burn them instead. The smoke which rises up will give you and my children great peace. Do not eat all of my flesh, but save a portion of it to plant in the ground the next year.'

The next morning, the husband did as First Mother had instructed and he killed her. According to her instructions, two men dragged her body over a fallow field until her flesh was all worn off, leaving them with her bones, which they buried.

After the passing of seven moons, her husband returned to the field where her body had been dragged and found it covered with beautiful green plants reaching to the sky. After removing the fruit of the plant and eating it, he discovered it to be sweet. He named the fruit Skar-mu-mal – 'corn'. In the middle of the field, where his wife's bones had been buried, he found another plant, this one shorter and with broad, brown leaves. Tasting it, he found it bitter. He named the plant Utar-mur-wa-yeh – 'tobacco'.

All the people of the village came out to the field and harvested the corn and the tobacco. Once the crops were gathered in, the people of the tribe called for help from Klos-kur-beh, who helped them divide their harvest evenly among them. When Klos-kur-beh arrived and found the great harvest in the field where First Mother had been dragged, he said: 'With this, the words of First Mother have been fulfilled. She claimed to have been born on the leaf of a beautiful plant. She said that she had the power to be loved by all people in the world and now so shall she be. Care well for the fruit of the green plants for they are the flesh of First Mother. Burn the other plant and the smoke will awaken your mind. These plants are filled with the goodness of the heart of First Mother. Remember her when you eat and when the smoke rises before you. Learn to share with one another, for then shall you know the love of the First Mother.'

THE MAGIC MOCCASINS

Passamaquoddy

THREE BROTHERS LIVED near the banks of a beautiful lake. Each of the three thought he was superior in all ways to his other two brothers. Sometimes the brothers were visited by an elderly woman who was nearly blind and could barely walk. She was always hungry. When the Old Woman had eaten, however, she could perform amazing things and could grant magical powers to anyone she fancied. The youngest of the three brothers, Joseph, treated the Old Woman well and he became one of her favourites. After he gave her a meal one day, she told him to take his axe and make a pair of wooden moccasins. 'Wear these,' she said to him, 'and you will run faster than any bird.' Joseph made himself such a pair of moccasins and, sure enough, when he put them on, he could run amazingly fast. He could outrun the fastest animals in the forest. He kept the Old Woman supplied with meat since he could easily outrun game animals and capture them with his hands.

When the other two brothers saw the gift of speed the Old Woman had given him, they were jealous. They did not know that his speed came from the wooden moccasins until they secretly watched him put them on in the forest when he thought he was alone.

Joseph kept his wooden moccasins in a birch-bark box. When his brothers found wooden chips where Joseph had carved his magic shoes, they gathered up the chips and made magical moccasins of their own. These moccasins allowed them to run faster than even Joseph! When Joseph saw his brothers in their wooden shoes, he knew they had spied on him and had come to know his secret.

When Joseph fed the Old Woman next, she thanked him by giving him instructions to carve a dug-out canoe. She promised that such a craft would allow him to glide through the water with great swiftness. Just as she told him, Joseph made the dug-out canoe. He was able to fly about the water in the canoe, catching many large fish and water-birds. Again his brothers were jealous of Joseph. They began to keep a close watch on him just as before and finally found some of the wooden chips made when Joseph carved his dug-out. The two brothers began to fashion their own canoe. It, too, was magical and even faster than Joseph's. With it they were able to catch even whales out in the mighty sea.

Joseph was angered by what his brothers had done and he met with the Old Woman, feeding her once again. She encouraged him to build another canoe. 'In this canoe,' she said, 'you will be able to fly through the sky as a bird.' Joseph built the new dug-out and, when he had completed his work, carefully gathered up the wooden chips and burned them all. Once he had completed his work, he sat in his new canoe and was soon flying off into the distant sky. Joseph flew over many new and wonderful lands, flying over strange places and watching strange people below. He travelled great distances, over tall mountains and great oceans. When he had completed his journeys, he returned to his village and there he lived at peace for the remainder of his days.

When the two brothers saw the gift of speed the Old Woman had given Joseph, they were jealous.

Source
John Prince, 'Notes on Passamaquoddy Literature', *Annals of the New York Academy of Science*, 23 (1901), 381–5; 11 (1898), pp. 369–75

THE STORY OF THE GREAT CHENOO

Micmac and Passamaquoddy

O F THE OLD TIME. An Indian, with his wife and their little boy, went one autumn far away to hunt in the northwest. And having found a fit place to pass the winter, they built a wigwam. The man brought home the game, the woman dressed and dried the meat, and the small boy played at shooting birds with bow and arrow; in Indian-wise all went well.

One afternoon, when the man was away and the wife gathering wood, she heard a rustling in the bushes, as though some beast were brushing through them, and, looking up, she saw with horror something worse than the worst she had feared. It was an awful face glaring at her – a something made of devil, man and beast in their most dreadful forms. It was like a haggard old man, with wolfish eyes; he was stark naked; his shoulders and lips were gnawed away, as if, when mad with hunger, he had eaten his own flesh. He carried a bundle on his back. The woman had heard of the terrible Chenoo, the being who comes from the far, icy north, a creature who is a man grown to be both devil and cannibal, and saw at once that this was one of them.

Truly she was in trouble; but dire need gives quick wit, as it was with this woman, who, instead of showing fear, ran up and addressed him with fair words, as 'My dear father', pretending surprise and joy, and, telling him how glad her heart was, asked where he had been so long. The Chenoo was amazed beyond measure at such a greeting where he expected yells and prayers, and in mute wonder let himself be led into the wigwam.

She was a wise and good woman. She took him in; she said she was sorry to see him so woebegone; she pitied his sad state; she brought a suit of her husband's clothes; she told him to dress himself and be cleaned. He did as she bade. He sat by the side of the wigwam, and looked surly and sad, but kept quiet. It was all a new thing to him.

She arose and went out. She kept gathering sticks. The Chenoo rose and followed her. She was in great fear. 'Now,' she thought, 'my death is near; now he will kill and devour me.'

The Chenoo came to her. He said, 'Give me the axe!' She gave it, and he began to cut down the trees. Man never saw such chopping! The great pines fell right and left, like summer saplings; the boughs were hewed and split as if by a tempest. She cried out, 'Noo, tabeagul boohsoogul! – My father, there is enough!' He laid down the axe; he walked into the wigwam and sat down, always in grim silence. The woman gathered her wood, and remained as silent on the opposite side.

She heard her husband coming. She ran out and told him all. She asked him to do as she was doing. He thought it well. He went in and spoke kindly. He said, 'N'chilch – My father-in-law', and asked where he had been so long. The Chenoo stared in amazement, but when he heard the man talk of all that had happened for years his fierce face grew gentler.

They had their meal; they offered him food, but he hardly touched it. He lay down to sleep. The man and his wife kept awake in terror. When the fire burned up and it became warm, the Chenoo asked that a screen should be placed before him. He was from the ice; he could not endure heat.

Source

Charles G. Leland, *The Algonquin Legends of New England*, Boston: Houghton, Mifflin, and Company, 1884, pp. 233–44

For three days he stayed in the wigwam; for three days he was sullen and grim; he hardly ate. Then he seemed to change. He spoke to the woman; he asked her if she had any tallow. She told him they had much. He filled a large kettle; there was a gallon in it. He put it on the fire. When it was scalding hot, he drank it all off at a draught.

He became sick; he grew pale. He cast up all the horrors and abominations of earth, things appalling to every sense. When all was over he seemed changed. He lay down and slept. When he awoke he asked for food and ate much. From that time he was kind and good. They feared him no more.

They lived on meat such as Indians prepare. The Chenoo was tired of it. One day he said, 'N'toos (my daughter), have you no *pela weoos*? (fresh meat)'. She said, 'No.' When her husband returned the Chenoo saw that there was black mud on his snow-shoes. He asked him if there was a spring of water near. The friend said there was one half a day's journey distant. 'We must go there tomorrow,' said the Chenoo.

And they went together, very early. The Indian was fleet in such running. But the old man, who seemed so wasted and worn, went on his snow-shoes like the wind. They came to the spring. It was large and beautiful; the snow was all melted away around it; the border was flat and green.

Then the Chenoo stripped himself and danced around the spring his magic dance; and soon the water began to foam, and anon to rise and fall, as if some monster below were heaving in accord with the steps and the song. The Chenoo danced faster and wilder; then the head of an immense *taktalok* (lizard) rose above the surface. The old man killed it with a blow of his hatchet. Dragging it out he began again to dance. He brought out another, the female, not so large, but still heavy as an elk. They were small spring lizards, but the Chenoo had conjured them; by his magic they were made into monsters.

He dressed the game; he cut it up. He took the heads and feet and tails and all that he did not want, and cast them back into the spring. 'They will grow again into many lizards,' he said. When the meat was trimmed it looked like that of the bear. He bound it together with withies; he took it on his shoulders; he ran like the wind; his load was nothing.

The Indian was a great runner; in all the land was not his like; but now he lagged far behind. 'Can you go no faster than that?' asked the Chenoo. 'The sun is setting; the red will be black soon. At this rate it will be dark before we get home. Get on my shoulders.'

The Indian mounted on the load. The Chenoo bade him hold his head low, so that he would not be knocked off by the branches. 'Brace your feet,' he asid, 'so as to be steady.' Then the old man flew like the wind – *nebe sokano'v'jal samastuk-teskugul chel wegwasumug wegul*; the bushes whistled as they flew past them. They got home before sunset.

Then the spring was at hand. One day the Chenoo told them that something terrible would soon come to pass. An enemy, a Chenoo, a woman, was coming like wind, yes – on the wind – from the north to kill him. There could be no escape from the battle. She would be far more furious, mad and cruel than any male, even one of his own cruel race, could be. He knew not how the battle would end; but the man and his wife must be put in a place of safety. To keep from hearing the terrible war-whoops of the Chenoo, which is death to mortals, their ears must be closed. They must hide themselves in a cave.

Then he sent the woman for the bundle which he had brought with him, and which had hung untouched on a branch of a tree since he had been with them. And he said if she found aught in it offensive to her to throw it away, but certainly to bring him a smaller bundle that was within the other. So she went and opened it, and that which she found therein was a pair of human legs and feet, the remains of some earlier horrid meal. She threw them far away. The small bundle she brought to him.

The Chenoo opened it and took from it a pair of horns – horns of the *chepitch-calm* (dragon). One of them has two branches; the other is straight and smooth. They were golden-bright. He gave the straight horn to the Indian; he kept the other. He said that these were magical weapons, and the only ones of any use in the coming fight. So they waited for the foe.

And the third day came. The Chenoo was fierce and bold; he listened; he had no fear. He heard the long and awful scream – like nothing of earth – of the enemy, as she sped through the air far away in the icy north, long ere the others could hear it. And the manner of it was this: that if they without harm should live after hearing the first deadly yell of the enemy they could take no harm, and if they did but hear the answering shout of their friend all would be well with them. But he said, 'Should you hear me call for help, then hasten with the horn, and you may save my life.'

They did as he bade: they stopped their ears; they hid in a deep hole dug in the ground. All at once the cry of the foe burst on them like screaming thunder; their ears rang with pain: they were well-nigh killed, for all the care they had taken. But then they heard the answering cry of their friend, and were no longer in danger from mere noise.

The battle begun, the fight was fearful. The monsters, by their magic with their rage, rose to the size of mountains. The tall pines were torn up, the ground trembled as in an earthquake, rocks crashed upon rocks, the conflict deepened and darkened; no tempest was ever so terrible. Then the male Chenoo was heard crying, '*N'loosook! choogooye! abog unumooe!* – My son-in-law, come and help me!'

He ran to the fight. What he saw was terrible! The Chenoos, who upright would have risen far above the clouds as giants of hideous form, were struggling on the ground. The female seemed to be the conqueror. She was holding her foe down, she knelt on him, she was doing all she could to thrust her dragon's horn into his ear. And he, to avoid death, was moving his head rapidly from side to side, while she, mocking his cries, said, 'You have no son-in-law to help you. – *Neen nabujjeole.* – I'll take your cursed life, and eat your liver.'

The Indian was so small by these giants that the stranger did not notice him. 'Now,' said his friend, 'thrust the horn into her ear!' He did this with a well-directed blow; he struck hard; the point entered her head. At the touch it sprouted quick as a flash of lightning, it darted through the head, it came out of the other ear, it had become like a long pole. It touched the ground, it struck downward, it took deep and firm root.

The male Chenoo bade him raise the other end of the horn and place it against a large tree. He did so. It coiled itself round the tree like a snake, it grew rapidly; the enemy was held hard and fast. Then the two began to dispatch her. It was long and weary work. Such a being, to be killed at all, must be hewed into small pieces; flesh and bones must all be utterly consumed by fire. Should the least fragment

'Now,' said the Chenoo, 'thrust the horn into her ear!'

remain unburnt, from it would spring a grown Chenoo, with all the force and fire of the first.

The fury of battle past, the Chenoos had become of their usual size. The victor hewed the enemy into small pieces, to be revenged for the insult and threat of eating his liver. He, having roasted that part of his captive, ate it before her; while she was yet alive he did this. He told her she was served as she would have served him.

But the hardest task of all was to come. It was to burn or melt the heart. It was of ice, and more than ice: as much colder as ice is colder than fire, as much harder as ice is harder than water. When placed in the fire it put out the flame, yet by long burning it melted slowly, until they at last broke it to fragments with a hatchet, and then melted these. So they returned to the camp.

Spring came. The snows of winter, as water, ran down the rivers to the sea; the ice and snow which had encamped on the inland hills sought the shore. So did the Indian and his wife; the Chenoo, with softened soul, went with them. Now he was becoming a man like other men. Before going they built a canoe for the old man: they did not cover it with birch bark; they made it of moose skin. In it they placed a part of their venison and skins. The Chenoo took his place in it; they took the lead, and he followed.

And after winding on with the river, down rapids and under forest boughs, they came out into the sunshine, on a broad, beautiful lake. But suddenly, when midway in the water, the Chenoo lay flat in the canoe, as if to hide himself. And to explain this he said that he had just then been discovered by another Chenoo, who was standing on the top of a mountain, whose dim blue outline could just be seen stretching far away to the north.

'He has seen me,' he said, 'but he cannot see you. Nor can he behold me now; but should he discover me again, his wrath will be roused. Then he will attack me; I know not who might conquer. I prefer peace.'

So he lay hidden, and they took his canoe in tow. But when they had crossed the lake and come to the river again, the Chenoo said that he could not travel further by water. He would walk the woods, but sail on streams no more. So they told him where they meant to camp that night. He started over mountains and through woods and up rocks, a far, roundabout journey. And the man and his wife went down the river in a spring freshet, headlong with the rapids. But when they had paddled round the point where they meant to pass the night, they saw smoke rising among the trees, and on landing they found the Chenoo sleeping soundly by the fire which had been built for them.

This he repeated for several days. But as they went south a great change came over him. He was a being of the north. Ice and snow had no effect on him, but he could not endure the soft airs of summer. He grew weaker and weaker; when they had reached their village he had to be carried like a little child. He had grown gentle. His fierce and formidable face was now like that of a man. His wounds had healed; his teeth no longer grinned wildly all the time. The people gathered round him in wonder.

He was dying. This was after the white men had come. They sent for a priest. He found the Chenoo as ignorant of all religion as a wild beast. At first he would repel the father in anger. Then he listened and learned the truth. So the old heathen's heart changed; he was deeply moved. He asked to be baptized, and as the first tear which he had ever shed in all his life came to his eyes he died.

HOW A MEDICINE MAN TURNED A MAN INTO A TREE

Passamaquoddy

THIS IS AN ANCIENT LEGEND concerning a Passamaquoddy woman who was always travelling through the forests. She ate many different varieties of tree and bush as she travelled until she became pregnant from eating one. As she grew larger with child, she stopped her forest travels and built herself a wigwam along the banks of a clear, swiftly running stream. Finally, one night, she gave birth to her child. Although her first thoughts were to kill the infant, she decided instead to make a small bark canoe and place her baby inside it. Then she set the canoe into the stream and watched as the canoe carried her child away. As the canoe floated out of sight, the child was safe inside. When the canoe floated alongside a village, one of the maidens discovered the canoe and found the baby inside. She took the baby home with her. Then something strange began to take place. Every morning in the village, a child died. No one could explain why this was happening.

Soon a curious woman watched as the rescued child toddled off each night to the river and returned soon afterwards. She watched the child closely and discovered that when he returned to his own wigwam, he was carrying a small tongue in his hand, which he roasted over a fire and ate. Only then did the child lie down to sleep for the night.

When, on the following morning, the word circulated throughout the village that another Indian child had died, the watchful woman spoke to the parents of the dead child, advising them to examine their child's mouth. Sure enough, the dead baby's tongue had been cut out, which had caused the baby to bleed to death.

Immediately, a tribal council was held to determine the fate of the young killer. Some wanted him cut to pieces and his body parts cast into the river, while others wished to burn the child until its body was nothing but ashes. While the council members deliberated, another child was killed by the rescued child, its tongue removed and roasted. Then the child promised everyone that he would murder no more children.

Then the child began mysteriously to grow so that he was suddenly a large boy. He told the people of the village that he intended to remove one of his own bones from his side. When he attempted this, all of his bones came tumbling out of his body at the same time. With his bones out of his body, the young boy began to grow very large.

In time, the young boy became a great medicine man of the Passamaquoddies. He had great gifts and powers which he used at the request of the villagers. When his tribe moved to another encampment site, he remained in the old one. Before moving, his people built him a new wigwam, where they continued to visit him even after they moved away from him. Usually, when he was visited by someone with a request for help, he would say to them, 'You must turn me over and examine me, for there you will find the medicine you need.'

One day, a young brave visited the Medicine Man, requesting a love elixir from him to attract a woman to him. The Medicine Man instructed the youth to turn him over. Underneath the Medicine Man lay an herb which the youth was told he must keep for ever.

Source
J. Walter Fewkes, 'How the Medicine Man was Born, and How He Turned a Man into a Tree', *JAFL*, 3 (1884), pp. 273–5

Immediately the young maidens of the camp began to follow the brave around. He found it impossible ever to be alone, due to the young women constantly giving him their attention. When the problem became too much for him, he returned to the Medicine Man and gave him back his herb.

A second young brave visited the Medicine Man, asking him for eternal life.

'Make me live as long as the earth exists,' he said to the conjuror.

The Medicine Man replied, 'What you have asked for is not easy, yet I shall endeavour to fulfil your request. Turn me over.'

The visitor found another herb beneath the Medicine Man. He ordered the brave to go at once to a site away from the encampment, a bare and barren place where no vegetation grew. The young warrior did as the conjuror instructed him, finding a destitute spot where no plants grew. As the youth stood on the spot, a change began to occur. He soon watched with horror as branches began to appear all over his body. Shortly, he was transformed into a cedar tree and doomed to stand on that spot, for ever, continuing to live without end, serving no good purpose for anyone.

HOW A YOUNG MAN DIED FROM LOVE

Passamaquoddy

O F THE OLDEN TIME. Two brothers went hunting in the autumn, and that as far as the head waters of the Penobscot, where they remained all winter. But in March their snow-shoes gave out, as did their moccasins, and they wished that a woman were there to mend them.

When the younger brother returned first to the lodge, the next day – which he generally did, to get it ready for the elder – he was astonished to find that someone had been there before him, and that, too, in the housekeeping. For garments had been mended, the place cleaned and swept, a fire built and the pot was boiling. He said nothing of this to his brother; but returning the next day at the same time, found that all had been attended to, as at first. And again he said nothing; but in the morning, when he went forth to hunt, he did but go a little way and, returning, watched, from a hidden place, the door. And there came a beautiful and graceful girl, well attired, who entered the wigwam. And he, stepping softly, looking through a hole in the hut, saw her very busy with her housekeeping.

Then he entered, and she seemed to be greatly alarmed and confused; but he calmed her, and they soon became good friends, sporting together very happily all day long like children, for indeed, they were both young.

When the sun's height was little and his shadows long, the girl said, 'I must go now. I hear your brother coming, and I fear him. But I will return tomorrow. Addio!'

So she went, and the elder brother knew nothing of what had happened. The next day she came again, and once more they played in sunshine and shadow until evening; but ere she went he sought to persuade her to remain always. And she, as if in doubt, answered, 'Tell thy brother all, and it may be that I will stay and serve ye both. For I can make the snow-shoes and moccasins which ye so much need,

Source
Charles G. Leland, *The Algonquin Legends of New England*, Boston: Houghton, Mifflin, and Company, 1884, pp. 295–9

and also canoes.' Then she departed with the day, and the elder, returning, heard from his brother all that had happened, and said, 'Truly I should be glad to have someone here to take care of the wigwam and make snow-shoes.'

So she came in the morning, and hearing from the younger that his brother had consented to her coming was very glad, and went away, as in haste. But she returned about noon, drawing a toboggin (sled) piled up with garments and arms, for she was a huntress. Indeed, she could do all things as few women could, whether it were cooking, needlework or making all that men need. And the winter passed very pleasantly, until the snow grew soft, and it was time for them to return. Till she came they had little luck in hunting, but since her coming all had gone well with them, and they now had a wonderful quantity of furs.

Then they returned in a canoe, going down the river to their village. But as they came near it the girl grew sad, for she had thrown out her soul to their home, though they knew it not, by means of a vision. And suddenly she said, as they came to a point of land, 'Here I must leave. I can go no further. Say nothing of me to your parents, for your father would have but little love for me.' And the young men sought to persuade her, but she only answered sorrowfully, 'It cannot be.' So they came home with their furs, and the elder was so proud of their luck and their strange adventure that he could not hold his peace, but told all.

Then his father was very angry, and said, 'All my life have I feared this. Know that this woman was a devil of the woods, a witch of the Mitche-hant, a sister of the Oonahgamess (goblins and ghosts).' And he spoke so earnestly and so long of this thing that they were afraid, and the elder, being persuaded by the sire, went forth to slay her, and the younger followed him afar. So they sought her by the stream, and found her bathing, and, seeing them, she ran up a little hill. And, as she ran, the elder shot an arrow at her. Then there was a strange flurry about her, a fluttering of scattered feathers, and they saw her fly away as a partridge. Returning, they told all this to their father, who said, 'You did well. I know all about these female devils who seek to destroy men. Verily this was a she-Mikumwess (prankster).'

But the younger could not forget her, and longed to see her again; so one day he went into the woods, and there he indeed found her, and she was as kind as before. Then he said, 'Truly it was not by my goodwill that my brother shot at you.' And she answered, 'Well do I know that, and that it was all by your father; yet I blame him not, for this is an affair of N'karnayoo, the days of old; and even yet it is not at an end, and the greatest is to come. But let the day be only a day unto itself; the things of tomorrow are for tomorrow, and those of yesterday are departed.' So they forgot their troubles, and played together merrily all day long in the woods and in the open places, and told stories of old times till sunset. And as the Kah-kah-goos, or Crow, went to his tree, the boy said, 'I must return'; and she replied, 'Whenever you would see me, come to the woods. And remember what I say. Do not marry anyone else. For your father wishes you to do so, and he will speak of it to you, and that soon. Yet it is for your sake only that I say this.' Then she told him word by word all that his father had said; but he was not astonished, for now he knew that she was not as other women; but he cared not. And he grew brave and bold, and then he was above all things. And when she told him that if he should marry another he would surely die, it was as nothing to him.

Then returning, the first thing his father said was, 'My son, I have provided a wife for you, and the wedding must be at once.' And he said, 'It is well. Let it be so.' Then the bride came. For four days they held the wedding dance; four days they feasted. But on the last day he said, 'This is the end of it all,' and he laid him down on a white bearskin, and a great sickness came upon him, and when they brought the bride to him he was dead.

Truly the father knew what ailed him, and more withal, of which he said nothing. But he liked the place no longer, and he and his went away therefrom, and scattered far and wide.

THE WOMAN AND THE SERPENT

Passamaquoddy

O F OLD TIMES. There was a very beautiful woman. She turned the heads of all the men. She married, and her husband died very soon after, but she immediately took another. Within a single year she had five husbands, and these were the cleverest and handsomest and bravest in the tribe. And then she married again.

This, the sixth, was such a silent man that he passed for a fool. But he was wiser than people thought. He came to believe, by thinking it over, that this woman had some strange secret. He resolved to find it out. So he watched her all the time. He kept his eye on her by night and by day.

It was summer, and she proposed to go into the woods to pick berries, and to camp there. By and by, when they were in the forest, she suggested that he should go on to the spot where they intended to remain and build a wigwam. He said that he would do so. But he went a little way into the woods and watched her.

As soon as she believed that he was gone, she rose and walked rapidly onwards. He followed her, unseen. She went on, till, in a deep, wild place among the rocks, she came to a pond. She sat down and sang a song. A great foam, or froth, rose to the surface of the water. Then in the foam appeared the tail of a serpent. The creature was of immense size. The woman, who had laid aside all her garments, embraced the serpent, which twined around her, enveloping all her limbs and body in his folds. The husband watched it all. He now understood that, the venom of the serpent having entered the woman, she had saved her life by transferring it to others, who died.

He went on to the camping ground and built a wigwam. He made up two beds; he built a fire. His wife came. She was earnest that there should be only a single bed. He sternly bade her lie by herself. She was afraid of him. She laid down and went to sleep. He arose three times during the night to replenish the fire. Every time he called her and there was no answer. In the morning he shook her. She was dead. She had died by the poison of the serpent. They sunk her in the pond where the snake lived.

Source
Charles G. Leland, *The Algonquin Legends of New England*, Boston: Houghton, Mifflin, and Company, 1884, pp. 273–5

THE ORIGIN OF INDIAN SUMMER

Penobscot

IN DAYS LONG PAST, as the Penobscot Indians say, an elderly man named Zuni paid a call to the Chief of the Sky Spirits requesting his aid. He had been ill in the spring of the year when all the others in his tribe were busying themselves with the planting of seeds. His illness had lingered and kept him from planting. By summer's end, the people of his village had harvested their corn and other vegetables. They had dried them for their winter's food. However, due to his illness, Zuni was not supplied with food for the cold, wintry season. He had nothing for his food.

In desperation, he visited the Chief of the Sky Spirits and spoke to him: 'I was ill when the spring planting was done and remained ill all summer. Now the harvest has come and gone and winter is approaching. I am not prepared. I have no food. I have come to you for help. What am I to do now?'

The Chief of the Sky Spirits took pity on the old man and gave him an immediate response. 'Although the season of planting and harvesting has passed, go, now, and plant your seeds. I will make certain that you will have food for the winter.'

With this advice and a promise from the Chief of the Sky Spirits, Zuni returned home and went immediately into his field and planted his seeds. Despite the fact that it was autumn, the season remained warm. No sooner had he finished his planting than the vegetables in his new garden were fully grown and ready for Zuni to begin harvesting. Within seven days, Zuni had gathered up all his new vegetables and his abundance was equal to any other man of his village. Only when he had completed his gathering did winter come.

Now the Penobscot people have a name for the warm days of autumn. They call them Indian summer.

Source
Frank G. Speck,
'Penobscot
Tales', *JAFL*, 48
(1935), pp. 95–6

GREAT HEAD AND THE TEN BROTHERS

Iroquois

FAR AWAY IN A REMOTE SPOT an orphaned family of ten boys lived with their uncle. The older brothers went out every day to hunt, but the younger ones, not yet fitted for so rigorous a life, remained at home with their uncle, or at least did not venture much beyond the immediate vicinity of their lodge. One day the hunters did not return at their usual hour. As the evening passed without bringing any sign of the missing youths, the little band at home became alarmed. At length the eldest of the boys left in the lodge volunteered to go in search of his brothers. His uncle consented, and he set off, but he did not return.

In the morning another brother said, 'I will go to seek my brothers.' Having obtained permission, he went, but he also did not come back. Another and another took upon himself the task of finding the lost hunters, but of the searchers as well as of those sought for there was no news forthcoming. At length only the youngest of the lads remained at home, and to his entreaties to be allowed to seek

Source
Lewis Spence,
*The Myths of the
North American
Indians*, London:
George G.
Harrap & Co.,
1914,
pp. 232–5

for his brothers the uncle turned a deaf ear, for he feared to lose the last of his young nephews.

One day when uncle and nephew were out in the forest the latter fancied he heard a deep groan, which seemed to proceed from the earth exactly under his feet. They stopped to listen. The sound was repeated – unmistakably a human groan. Hastily they began digging in the earth, and in a moment or two came upon a man covered with mould and apparently unconscious.

The pair carried the unfortunate one to their lodge, where they rubbed him with bear's oil till he recovered consciousness. When he was able to speak he could give no explanation of how he came to be buried alive. He had been out hunting, he said, when suddenly his mind became a blank, and he remembered nothing more till he found himself in the lodge with the old man and the boy. His hosts begged the stranger to stay with them, and they soon discovered that he was no ordinary mortal, but a powerful magician. At times he behaved very strangely. One night, while a great storm raged without, he tossed restlessly on his couch instead of going to sleep. At last he sought the old uncle.

'Do you hear that noise?' he said. 'That is my brother, Great Head, who is riding on the wind. Do you not hear him howling?'

The old man considered this astounding speech for a moment, then he asked, 'Would he come here if you sent for him?'

'No,' said the other, thoughtfully, 'but we might bring him here by magic. Should he come you must have food ready for him, in the shape of huge blocks of maple wood, for that is what he lives on.'

The stranger departed in search of his brother Great Head, taking with him his bow, and on the way he came across a hickory tree, whose roots provided him with arrows. About midday he drew near to the dwelling of his brother, Great Head. In order to see without being seen, he changed himself into a mole, and crept through the grass till he saw Great Head perched on a rock, frowning fiercely. 'I see thee!' he growled, with his wild eyes fixed on an owl. The man-mole drew his bow and shot an arrow at Great Head. The arrow became larger and larger as it flew towards the monster, but it returned to him who had fired it, and as it did so it regained its natural size. The man seized it and rushed back the way he had come. Very soon he heard Great Head in pursuit, puffing and snorting along on the wings of a hurricane. When the creature had almost overtaken him he turned and discharged another arrow. Again and again he repulsed his pursuer in this fashion, till he lured him to the lodge where his benefactors lived. When Great Head burst into the house the uncle and nephew began to hammer him vigorously with mallets. To their surprise the monster broke into laughter, for he had recognized his brother and was very pleased to see him. He ate the maple blocks they brought him with a hearty appetite, whereupon they told him the story of the missing hunters.

'I know what has become of them,' said Great Head. 'They have fallen into the hands of a witch. If this young man –' indicating the nephew – 'will accompany me, I will show him her dwelling, and the bones of his brothers.'

The youth, who loved adventure, and was besides very anxious to learn the fate of his brothers, at once consented to seek the home of the witch. So he and Great Head started off, and lost no time in getting to the place. They found the space in front of the lodge strewn with dry bones, and the witch sitting in the doorway singing. When she saw them she muttered the magic word, which turned living

The youth, who loved adventure, and was besides very anxious to learn the fate of his brothers, at once consented to seek the home of the witch.

people into dry bones, but on Great Head and his companion it had no effect whatever. Acting on a prearranged signal, Great Head and the youth attacked the witch and killed her. No sooner had she expired than her flesh turned into birds and beasts and fishes. What was left of her they burned to ashes.

Their next act was to select the bones of the nine brothers from among the heap, and this they found no easy task. But at last it was accomplished, and Great Head said to his companion, 'I am going home to my rock. When I pass overhead in a great storm I will bid these bones arise, and they will get up and return with you.'

The youth stood alone for a little while till he heard the sound of a fierce tempest. Out of the hurricane Great Head called to the brothers to arise. In a moment they were all on their feet, receiving the congratulations of their younger brother and each other, and filled with joy at their reunion.

THE WOMAN WHO MARRIED THE THUNDER

Passamaquoddy

ONCE A WOMAN WENT to the edge of a lake and lay down to sleep. As she awoke, she saw a great serpent, with glittering eyes, crawl from the water and stealthily approach her. She had no power to resist his embrace. After her return to her people her condition betrayed itself and she was much persecuted; they pursued her with sticks and stones, howling abuse.

She fled from the village, she went afar into wild places, and, sitting down on the grass, wept, wishing that she were dead. As she sat and wailed, a very beautiful girl, dressed in silver and gold, appeared and, after listening to her sad story, said, 'Follow me!'

They came into a pleasant wigwam with a very smooth floor. An old man, so old that he was all white, came to meet them.

Then they went up high into a mountain, through three rocks, until they came into a pleasant wigwam with a very smooth floor. An old man, so old that he was all white, came to meet them. Then he, taking a short stick, bade her dance. He began to sing, and as he sang she gave birth, one by one, to twelve serpents. These the old man killed in succession with his stick as they were born. Then she became thin again and was in her natural form.

The old man had a son, Badawk, the Thunder, and a daughter, Psawk-tankapic, the Lightning, and when Thunder returned he offered to take her back to her own people, but she refused to go. Then the old man said to his son, 'Take her for your wife and be good to her.' So they were married.

In time she bore a son. When the boy could stand, the old man, who never leaves the mountain, called him to stand before him, while he fastened wings to the child. He was soon able, with these wings, to make a noise, which greatly pleased the grandfather. When a storm is approaching, the distant rumbling is the muttering thunder made by the child, but it is Badawk, his father, who comes in the dark cloud and makes the roaring crash, while Psawk-tankapic flashes her lightnings.

In after-days, when the woman visited her people, she told them that they never need fear the thunder or lightning.

Source

George G. Leland, *The Algonquin Legends of New England*, Boston: Houghton, Mifflin, and Company, 1884, pp. 266–7

THE BOY MAGICIAN

Iroquois

IN THE HEART OF THE WILDERNESS there lived an old woman and her little grandson. The two found no lack of occupation from day to day, the woman busying herself with cooking and cleaning and the boy with shooting and hunting. The grandmother frequently spoke of the time when the child would grow up and go out into the world.

'Always go to the east,' she would say. 'Never go to the west, for there lies danger.'

But what the danger was she would not tell him, in spite of his inportunate questioning. Other boys went west, he thought to himself, and why should not he? Nevertheless his grandmother made him promise that he would not go west.

Years passed by and the child grew to be a man, though he still retained the curiosity and high spirits of his boyhood. His persistent inquiries drew from the old grandmother a reluctant explanation of her warning.

'In the west,' said she, 'there dwells a being who is anxious to do us harm. If he sees you it will mean death for both of us.'

This statement, instead of frightening the young Indian, only strengthened in him a secret resolution he had formed to go west at the first opportunity. Not that he wished to bring any misfortune on his poor old grandmother, any more than on himself, but he trusted to his strong arm and clear head to deliver them from their enemy. So with a laugh on his lips he set off to the west.

Towards evening he came to a lake, where he rested. He had not been there long when he heard a voice saying, 'Aha, my fine fellow, I see you!'

The youth looked all round him, and up into the sky above, but he saw no one.

'I am going to send a hurricane,' the mysterious voice continued, 'to break your grandmother's hut to pieces. How will you like that?'

'Oh, very well,' answered the young man gaily. 'We are always in need of firewood, and now we shall have plenty.'

'Go home and see,' the voice said mockingly. 'I dare say you will not like it so well.'

Nothing daunted, the young adventurer retraced his steps. As he neared home a great wind sprang up, seeming to tear the very trees out by the roots.

'Make haste!' cried the grandmother from the doorway. 'We shall both be killed!'

When she had drawn him inside and shut the door she scolded him heartily for his disobedience, and bewailed the fate before them. The young man soothed her fears, saying, 'Don't cry, grandmother. We shall turn the lodge into a rock, and so we shall be saved.'

Having some skill in magic, he did as he had said, and the hurricane passed harmlessly over their heads. When it had ceased, they emerged from their retreat, and found an abundance of firewood all round them.

Next day the youth was on the point of setting off towards the west once more, but the urgent entreaties of his grandmother moved him to proceed eastward – for a time. Directly he was out of sight of the lodge he turned his face once more to the west. Arrived at the lake, he heard the voice once more, though its owner was still invisible.

Source
Lewis Spence,
The Myths of the North American Indians, London: George G. Harrap & Co., 1914, pp. 238–42

'I am going to send a great hailstorm on your grandmother's hut,' it said. 'What do you think of that?'

'Oh,' was the response, 'I think I should like it. I have always wanted a bundle of spears.'

'Go home and see,' said the voice.

Away the youth went through the woods. The sky became darker and darker as he neared his home, and just as he was within a bowshot of the little hut a fierce hailstorm broke and he thought he would be killed before he was able to reach shelter.

'Alas!' cried the old woman when he was safely indoors. 'We shall be destroyed this time. How can we save ourselves?'

Again the young man exercised his magic powers, and transformed the frail hut into a hollow rock, upon which the shafts of the hailstorm spent themselves in vain. At last the sky cleared, the lodge resumed its former shape, and the young man saw a multitude of sharp, beautiful spear-heads on the ground.

'I will get poles,' said he, 'to fit to them for fishing.'

When he returned in a few minutes with the poles he found that the spears had vanished.

'Where are my beautiful spears?' he asked his grandmother.

'They were only ice-spears,' she replied. 'They have all melted away.'

The young Indian was greatly disappointed, and wondered how he could avenge himself on the being who had played on him this malicious trick.
'Be warned in time,' said the aged grandmother, shaking her head at him. 'Take my advice and leave him alone.'

But the youth's adventurous spirit impelled him to see the end of the matter, so he took a stone and tied it round his neck for a charm, and sought the lake once again. Carefully observing the direction from which the voice proceeded, he saw in the middle of the lake a huge head with a face on every side of it.

'Aha, uncle!' he exclaimed, 'I see you! How would you like it if the lake dried up?'

'Nonsense!' said the voice angrily. 'That will never happen.'

'Go home and see,' shouted the youth, mimicking the mocking tone the other had adopted on the previous occasions. As he spoke he swung his charmed stone round his head and threw it into the air. As it descended it grew larger and larger, and the moment it entered the lake the water began to boil.

The lad returned home and told his grandmother what he had done.

'It is of no use,' said she. 'Many have tried to slay him, but all have perished in the attempt.'

Next morning our hero went westward again, and found the lake quite dry and the animals in it dead, with the exception of a large green frog, who was in reality the malicious being who had tormented the Indian and his grandmother. A quick blow with a stick put an end to the creature, and the triumphant youth bore the good news back to his old grandmother, who from that time was left in peace and quietness.

THE FRIENDLY SKELETON

Iroquois

ALITTLE BOY LIVING in the woods with his old uncle was warned by him not to go eastward, but to play close to the lodge or walk towards the west. The child felt a natural curiosity to know what lay in the forbidden direction, and one day took advantage of his uncle's absence on a hunting expedition to wander away to the east. At length he came to a large lake, on the shores of which he stopped to rest. Here he was accosted by a man, who asked him his name and where he lived.

'Come,' said the stranger, when he had finished questioning the boy, 'let us see who can shoot an arrow the highest.'

This they did, and the boy's arrow went much higher than that of his companion. The stranger then suggested a swimming match.

'Let us see,' he said, 'who can swim farthest under water without taking a breath.'

Again the boy beat his rival, who next proposed that they should sail out to an island in the middle of the lake, to see the beautiful birds that were to be found there. The child consented readily, and they embarked in a curious canoe, which was propelled by three swans harnessed to either side of it. Directly they had taken their seats the man began to sing, and the canoe moved off. In a very short time, they had reached the island. Here the little Indian realized that his confidence in his new-found friend was misplaced. The stranger took all his clothes from him, put them in the canoe and jumped in himself, saying, 'Come, swans, let us go home.'

The obedient swans set off at a good pace, and soon left the island far behind. The boy was very angry at having been so badly used, but when it grew dark his resentment changed to fear, and he sat down and cried with cold and misery. Suddenly he heard a husky voice close at hand, and, looking round, he saw a skeleton on the ground.

'I am very sorry for you,' said the skeleton in hoarse tones. 'I will do what I can to help you. But first you must do something for me. Go and dig by that tree, and you shall find a tobacco pouch with some tobacco in it, a pipe and a flint.'

The boy did as he was asked, and when he had filled the pipe he lit it and placed it in the mouth of the skeleton. He saw that the latter's body was full of mice, and that the smoke frightened them away.

'There is a man coming tonight with three dogs,' said the skeleton. 'He is coming to look for you. You must make tracks all over the island, so that they may not find you, and then hide in a hollow tree.'

Again the boy obeyed his gaunt instructor, and when he was safely hidden he saw a man come ashore with three dogs. All night they hunted him, but he had made so many tracks that the dogs were confused, and at last the man departed in anger. Next day the trembling boy emerged and went to the skeleton.

'Tonight,' said the latter, 'the man who brought you here is coming to drink your blood. You must dig a hole in the sand and hide. When he comes out of the canoe you must enter it. Say, "Come, swans, let us go home," and if the man calls you do not look back.'

They sailed to an island in the middle of the lake in a curious canoe propelled by three swans harnessed to either side of it.

Source

Lewis Spence, *The Myths of the North American Indians*, London: George G. Harrap & Co., 1914, pp. 227–32

Everything fell out as the skeleton had foretold. The boy hid in the sand, and directly he saw his tormentor step ashore he jumped into the canoe, saying hastily, 'Come, swans, let us go home.' Then he began to sing as he had heard the man do when they first embarked. In vain the man called him back; he refused to look round. The swans carried the canoe to a cave in a high rock, where the boy found his clothes, as well as a fire and food. When he had donned his garments and satisfied his hunger he lay down and slept. In the morning he returned to the island, where he found the tyrant quite dead. The skeleton now commanded him to sail eastward to seek for his sister, whom a fierce man had carried away. He set out eagerly on his new quest, and a three days' journey brought him to the place where his sister was. He lost no time in finding her.

'Come, my sister,' said he, 'let us flee away together.'

'Alas! I cannot,' answered the young woman. 'A wicked man keeps me here. It is time for him to return home, and he would be sure to catch us. But let me hide you now, and in the morning we shall go away.'

So she dug a pit and hid her brother, though not a moment too soon, for the footsteps of her husband were heard approaching the hut. The woman had cooked a child, and this she placed before the man.

'You have had visitors,' he said, seeing his dogs snuffing around uneasily.

'No,' was the reply, 'I have seen no one but you.'

'I shall wait till tomorrow,' said the man to himself. 'Then I shall kill and eat him.' He had already guessed that his wife had not spoken the truth. However, he said nothing more, but waited till morning, when, instead of going to a distant swamp to seek for food, as he pretended to do, he concealed himself at a short distance from the hut, and at length saw the brother and sister making for a canoe. They were hardly seated when they saw him running towards them. In his hand he bore a large hook, with which he caught the frail vessel; but the lad broke the hook with a stone, and the canoe darted out on to the lake. The man was at a loss for a moment, and could only shout incoherent threats after the pair. Then an idea occurred to him, and, lying down on the shore, he began to drink the water. This caused the canoe to rush back again, but once more the boy was equal to the occasion. Seizing the large stone with which he had broken the hook, he threw it at the man and slew him, the water at the same time rushing back into the lake. Thus the brother and sister escaped, and in three days they had arrived at the island, where they heartily thanked their benefactor, the skeleton. He, however, had still another task for the young Indian to perform.

'Take your sister home to your uncle's lodge,' said he, 'then return here yourself, and say to the many bones which you will find on the island, "Arise," and they shall come to life again.'

When the brother and sister reached their home they found that their old uncle had been grievously lamenting the loss of his nephew, and he was quite overjoyed at seeing them. On his recommendation they built a large lodge to accommodate the people they were to bring back with them. When it was completed, the youth revisited the island, bade the bones arise, and was delighted to see them obey his bidding and become men and women. He led them to the lodge he had built, where they all dwelt happily for a long time.

The Young Man Who was Saved by a Rabbit and a Fox

Passamaquoddy

THERE DWELT A COUPLE in the woods, far away from other people – a man and his wife. They had one boy, who grew up strong and clever. One day he said, 'Father and mother, let me go and see other men and women.' They grieved, but let him go.

He went afar. All night he lay on the ground. In the morning he heard something coming. He rose and saw it was a Rabbit, who said, 'Ha, friend, where go you?'

The boy answered, 'To find people.'

'That is what I want,' replied the Rabbit. 'Let us go together.'

So they went on for a long time, till they heard voices far off, and walking quietly came to a village.

'Now,' said the Rabbit, 'steal up unseen and listen to them!' The boy did so, and heard the people saying that a *kewahqu'* 'a cannibal monster', was to come the next day to devour the daughter of their sagamore. And having returned and reported this to the Rabbit, the latter said to the boy, 'Have no fear; go to the people and tell them that you can save her.' He did so, but it was long before they would listen to him. Yet at last it came to the ears of the old chief that a strange young man insisted that he could save the girl; so the chief sent for him, and said, 'They tell me that you think you can deliver my daughter from death. Do so and she shall be yours.'

Then he returned to the Rabbit, who said, 'They did not send the girl far away because they know that the demon can follow any track. But I hope to make a track which he cannot follow. Now do you, as soon as it shall be dark, bring her to this place.'

The young man did so, and the Rabbit was there with a sled, and in his hand he had two squirrels. These he smoothed down, and as he did so they grew to be as large as the largest sled-dogs. Then all three went headlong, like the wind, till they came to another village.

The Rabbit looked about till he found a certain wigwam and then peered through a crevice into it. 'This is the place,' he said. 'Enter.' They did so; then the Rabbit ran away. They found in the cabin an old woman, who was very kind, but who, on seeing them, burst into tears. 'Ah, my dear grandchildren,' she cried, 'your death is following you rapidly, for the *kewahqu'* is on your track and will soon be here. But run down to the river, where you will find your grandfather camping.'

They went and were joined by the Rabbit, who had spent the time in making many divergent tracks in the ground. The *kewahqu'* came. The tracks delayed him a long time, but at last he found the right one. Meanwhile, the young couple went on, and found an old man by the river. He said, 'Truly you are in great danger, for the *kewahqu'* is coming. But I will help you.' Saying this, he threw himself into the water, where he floated with outstretched limbs, and said, 'Now, my children, get on me.' The girl feared lest she should fall off, but being reassured mounted, when he turned into a canoe, which carried them safely across. But when they turned to look at him, lo! he was no longer a canoe, but an old Duck. 'Now, my dear children,' he said, 'hasten to the top of yonder grey mountain.' The *kewahqu'* came

Source
Charles G. Leland, *The Algonquin Legends of New England*, Boston: Houghton, Mifflin, and Company, 1884, pp. 227–32

raging and roaring in a fury, but however he pursued, they were at the foot of the precipice before him.

There stood the Rabbit. He was holding up a very long pole; no pine was ever longer. 'Climb this,' he said. And, as they climbed, it lengthened, till they left it for the hill, and then scrambled up the rocks. Then the *kewahqu'* came yelling and howling horribly. Seeing the fugitives far above, he swarmed up the pole. With him, too, it grew, and grew rapidly, till it seemed to be half a mile high. Now the *kewahqu'* was no such sorcerer that he could fly; neither had he wings; he must remain on the pole; and when he came to the top the young man pushed it afar. It fell, and the monster was killed by the fall thereof.

They went with the squirrel-sledge; they flew through the woods on the snow by the moonlight; they were very glad. And at last they came to the girl's village, when the Rabbit said, 'Now, friend, goodbye. Yet there is more trouble coming, and when it is with you I and mine will aid you. So farewell.' And when they were home again it all appeared like a dream. Then the wedding feast was held, and all seemed well.

But the young men of the village hated the youth, and desired to kill him that they might take his wife. They persuaded him to go with them fishing on the sea. Then they raised a cry, and said, 'A whale is chasing us! He is under the canoe!' and suddenly they knocked him overboard, and paddled away like an arrow in flight.

The young man called for help. A Crow came, and said, 'Swim or float as long as you can. I will bring you aid.' He floated a long time. The Crow returned with a strong cord; the Crow made himself very large; he threw one end of the cord to the youth; by the other he towed him to a small island. 'I can do no more,' he said, 'but there is another friend.' So as the youth sat there, starving and freezing, there came to him a Fox.

'Ha, friend,' he said, 'are you here?'

'Yes,' replied the youth, 'and dying of hunger.'

The Fox reflected an instant, and said, 'Truly I have no meat; and yet there is a way.' So he picked from the ground a blade of dry grass, and bade the youth eat it. He did so, and found himself a moose (or a horse). Then he fed richly on the young grass till he had enough, when the Fox gave him a second straw, and he became a man again.

'Friend,' said the Fox, 'there is an Indian village on the mainland, where there is to be a great feast, a grand dance. Would you like to be there?'

'Indeed I would,' replied the youth.

'Then wait till dark, and I will take you there,' said the Fox. And when night came he bade the youth close his eyes and enter the river, and take hold of the end of his tail, while he should draw. So in the tossing sea they went on for hours.

Thought the youth, 'We shall never get there.'

Said the Fox, 'Yes, we will, but keep your eyes shut.'

So it went on for another hour, when the youth thought again, 'We shall never reach land.'

Said the Fox, 'Yes, we shall.' However, after a time he opened his eyes, when they were only ten feet from the shore, and this cost them more time and trouble than all the previous swim ere they had the beach underfoot.

It was his own village. The festival was for the marriage of his own wife to one of the young men who had pushed him overboard. Great was his magic power,

They went with the squirrel sledge, flying through the woods on the snow by the moonlight.

great was his anger; he became strong as death. Then he went to his own wigwam, and his wife, seeing him, cried aloud for joy, and kissed him and wept all at once. He said, 'Be glad, but the hour of punishment for the men who made these tears is come.' So he went to the sagamore and told him all.

The old chief called for the young men. 'Slay them all as you choose,' he said to his son-in-law; 'scalp them.' But the youth refused. He called to the Fox and got the straws which gave the power to transform men to beasts. He changed his enemies into bad animals – one into a porcupine, one into a hog – and they were driven into the woods. Thus it was that the first hog and the first porcupine came into the world.

GLOOSCAP THE DIVINITY

Wabanaki

NOW THE GREAT LORD GLOOSCAP, who was worshipped in after-days by all the Wabanaki, or the children of light, was a twin with a brother. As he was good, this brother, whose name was Malsumsis, or Wolf the younger, was bad. Before they were born, the babes consulted to consider how they had best enter the world. And Glooscap said, 'I will be born as others are.' But the evil Malsumsis thought himself too great to be brought forth in such a manner, and declared that he would burst through his mother's side. As they planned it so it came to pass. Glooscap as first came quietly to light, while Malsumsis kept his word, killing his mother.

The two grew up together, and one day the younger, who knew that both had charmed lives, asked the elder what would kill him, Glooscap. Now each had his own secret as to this, and Glooscap, remembering how wantonly Malsumsis had slain their mother, thought it would be misplaced confidence to trust his life to one so fond of death, while it might prove to be well to know the bane of the other. So they agreed to exchange secrets, and Glooscap, to test his brother, told him that the only way in which he himself could be slain was by the stroke of an owl's feather, though this was not true. And Malsumsis said, 'I can die only by a blow from a fern-root.'

It came to pass in after-days that Kwah-beet-a-sis, the son of the Great Beaver, or, as others say, Miko the Squirrel, or else the evil which was in himself, tempted Malsumsis to kill Glooscap; for in those days all men were wicked. So taking his bow he shot Ko-ko-khas the Owl, and with one of his feathers he struck Glooscap while sleeping. Then he awoke in anger, yet craftily said that it was not by an owl's feather, but by a blow from a pine-root, that his life would end.

Then the false man led his brother another day far into the forest to hunt, and, while he again slept, smote him on the head with a pine-root. But Glooscap arose unharmed, drove Malsumsis away into the woods, sat down by the brook-side and, thinking over all that had happened, said, 'Nothing but a flowering rush can kill me.' But the Beaver, who was hidden among the reeds, heard this, and hastening to Malsumsis told him the secret of his brother's life. For this Malsumsis promised to bestow on Beaver whatever he should ask; but when the latter wished for wings

Source
Charles G.
Leland, *The
Algonquin
Legends of New
England*, Boston:
Houghton,
Mifflin, and
Company, 1884,
pp. 15–17

like a pigeon, the warrior laughed and scornfully said, 'Get thee hence; thou with a tail like a file, what need hast thou of wings?'

Then the Beaver was angry, and went forth to the camp of Glooscap, to whom he told what he had done. Therefore Glooscap arose in sorrow and in anger, took a fern-root, sought Malsumsis in the deep, dark forest and smote him so that he fell down dead. And Glooscap sang a song over him and lamented.

How Glooscap Caught the Summer

Algonquin

A LONG TIME AGO Glooscap wandered very far north to the Ice-country, and, feeling tired and cold, sought shelter at a wigwam where dwelt a great giant – the giant Winter. Winter received the god hospitably, filled a pipe of tobacco for him and entertained him with charming stories of the old time as he smoked. All the time Winter was casting his spell over Glooscap, for as he talked drowsily and monotonously, he gave forth a freezing atmosphere, so that Glooscap first dozed and then fell into a deep sleep – the heavy slumber of the winter season. For six whole months he slept; then the spell of the frost arose from his brain and he awoke. He took his way homeward and southward, and the farther south he fared the warmer it felt, and the flowers began to spring up around his steps.

At length he came to a vast, trackless forest, where, under primeval trees, many little people were dancing. The queen of these folk was Summer, a most exquisitely beautiful, if very tiny, creature. Glooscap caught the queen up in his great hand and, cutting a long lasso from the hide of a moose, secured it round her tiny frame. Then he ran away, letting the cord trail loosely behind him.

The tiny people, who were the Elves of Light, came clamouring shrilly after him, pulling frantically at the lasso. But as Glooscap ran the cord ran out, and pull as they might they were left far behind.

Northward he journeyed once more, and came to the wigwam of Winter. The giant again received him hospitably, and began to tell the old stories whose vague charm had exercised such a fascination upon the god. But Glooscap in his turn began to speak. Summer was lying in his bosom, and her strength and heat sent forth such powerful magic that at length Winter began to show signs of distress. The sweat poured profusely down his face, and gradually he commenced to melt, as did his dwelling. Then slowly nature awoke, the song of birds was heard, first faintly, then more clearly and joyously. The thin green shoots of the young grass appeared, and the dead leaves of last autumn were carried down to the river by the melting snow. Lastly the fairies came out, and Glooscap, leaving Summer with them, once more bent his steps southward.

Source
Lewis Spence,
The Myths of the North American Indians, London: George G. Harrap & Co., 1914, pp. 147–9

PART 2
THE SOUTHEAST

TRIBES OF THE SOUTHEAST

The Southeastern region of the United States was the homeland of a wide variety of Indian tribes prior to the coming of Europeans to the New World. This vast setting, which stretched east and west from the Atlantic coast to the Mississippi River and north and south from the Ohio River to the Gulf of Mexico, witnessed the comings and goings of several variant language families. The primary language stock of these Southeastern tribes was the Muskogean branch. Tribes who spoke a dialect rooted in this language source included the Creeks, Hitchitis and Yamasees of modern Georgia; the Seminoles in Florida; the Chickasaws, Choctaws and Houmas of Mississippi; and the Alabamas and Mobiles of the state named after the former. Other less well-known tribes of the Muskogean family included the Timucuas of northern, coastal Florida and the Calusas of the southern Florida peninsula.

Yet despite the predominance of Indians of a Muskogean-based tongue in the Southeast, other native groups, speaking other language stocks, were located in the region. Perhaps the largest and most readily known group were the Cherokees, who ranged through North Carolina and Tennessee. They spoke a language based on Iroquois stock. In Mississippi, the Biloxi tribal language was Siouan in origin, as was also that of the Yuchis, whose traditional lands were located in northern Georgia.

Most of these tribes were located on their traditional lands before the arrival of the first Europeans and their cultures were firmly fixed historically. Pottery had been produced by most of these tribes for over 3,000 years. Around AD 700, an extremely dominant culture arose in the Southeast, which archaeologists refer to as the Mississippian Culture or the Middle Mississippian. It developed along the banks of several key Southeastern river systems, including the Illinois, Tennessee, the lower Ohio and the middle Mississippi. How exactly this culture developed is unclear, but many anthropologists consider the Mississippians to embody the third era of what has come to be known by archaeologists as the mound-builders.

Mound-building was a practice of various native cultures in the Southeast dating back thousands of years. The original mound-builders, who practised this earthen architecture from around 2,500 years ago, are referred to as the Adenas, a name that derives from the region in Ohio where early Indian mounds were discovered. The Adenas constructed cone-shaped mounds of earth, burying their dead in an above-ground earthen mound. Some of their early mounds were constructed in the shapes of animals, such as bears, frogs and birds.

The second phase of mound-building is known as the Hopewell era, which began about 2,000 years ago. The name is derived from the mounds uncovered in the nineteenth century on an Ohio farm located in Ross County and owned by M.C. Hopewell. At his request, archaeologists were allowed to dig into nearly three dozen such mounds on his property, in which they unearthed a variety of relics, including utensils and bones of local origin. However, the mounds also revealed the extensive trade contacts of these ancient Indians as they contained Atlantic coastal shells, bracelets, earrings and breastplates made from copper mined in the Lake Superior region and obsidian fragments from west of the Mississippi River.

The Hopewell Culture practised the architecture of constructing mounds on a greater scale than their predecessors did. Their mounds were larger, and the contents discovered by archaeologists reveal more wealthy societies than those common to the Adenas. In addition, their mounds were more elaborate, consisting of earth-works that involve intricate patterns of circles, squares, rectangles and octagons. Some mound systems stretched for three or four miles (five or six kilometres) in length. Construction of such mounds would have required the recruitment of a vast workforce, pressed into labour by a powerful centralized government.

By AD 700, or perhaps a century or so earlier, the third phase of mound-building began to develop. The Mississippian Culture serves historically as the immediate predecessor of the more modern tribes, such as the Choctaws, Chickasaws, Natchez and others. This culture was centred in the Southeastern states of Mississippi, Alabama and Tennessee.

Perhaps the most recognizable change in the Mississippi mound-building from that of the Hopewell and the Adenas was the construction of earthen pyramids. While earlier mounds were seemingly constructed as burial sites, the Mississippian pyramids served as temples and, occasionally, as the base for a chieftain's dwelling.

During the Mississippian phase, corn was introduced from Mexico, and the Indians began developing a serious agriculture. As a result of this sedentary culture, native cities began to develop, such as the impressive city of Cahokia, located in the region where the Mississippi and Missouri rivers join one another. Cahokia was situated on the eastern bank of the Mississippi River, opposite modern-day St Louis. It covered six square miles (more than fifteen square kilometres) and boasted an ancient population of approximately 25,000 people. Archaeologists have unearthed at least eighty-five mounds at this Mississippian site. Considering that this culture did not have a practical use of the wheel or animals to carry heavy loads, this building accomplishment is stupendous. The mounds were created by the labours of thousands of workers, who carried baskets of earth up the incline, depositing their load at the mound's ever-increasing summit. Over time, the city declined and was eventually abandoned. The reasons for its collapse as an ancient population centre are not clear.

The Mississippian stage of mound-building had reached its peak during the 1500s. As these large, sedentary centres, such as Cahokia, fell apart, the people scattered and dispersed into smaller tribal units, remaining largely agricultural and, to an extent, still village-oriented.

The Survival of the Natchez Culture

One mound culture that did survive until the arrival of the Europeans was that of the Natchez. By the time of the Spanish explorer DeSoto arrived on the lower Mississippi in the 1540s, the Natchez numbered about 4,000 natives living in at least nine town settlements scattered along the river. Such villages were ruled, even by the final decades of the 1600s, by a powerful chief known as the Great Sun. The village where the Great Sun lived was known as the Great Village, near modern-day Natchez, Mississippi. The tribal belief was that the chief was a descendant of the sun and he was treated with a deference often associated with that given to Aztec or Inca rulers.

Below this nobility in the Natchez Culture were the common people, referred to by contemporary French explorers and missionaries of the day as 'Stinkards'. While these two castes were tightly drawn, they did have significant contact with one another. Records indicate that by tribal law all noblewomen who married had to marry a Stinkard. Their children were considered aristocracy. However, a nobleman who married a Stinkard woman produced Stinkard children. This fact indicates that the blood lines were traced through the female, creating a matrilineal structure. The Natchez Culture did not survive white contact – the last remnants of the mound-building culture in the American Southeast.

Daily Life Among the Natchez

The Natchez were a settled, agricultural society. Their chief crop was corn, yet their diet was as varied as that of many of the Northeastern tribes. In addition, they harvested wild river rice and gathered a wide variety of edible seeds. Hunting provided meat for their diets. Contact with the Spanish and French introduced new foods to the Natchez. In fact, over time, especially after contact with Europeans, the Natchez named their lunar months of the year after important crops, foods and animals. In order, the list of months was as follows: Deer, Strawberries, Little Corn, Watermelons, Peaches, Mulberries, Great Corn, Turkeys, Bison, Bears, Cold Meal, Chestnuts and Nuts. (Items such as watermelons and peaches had European origins.)

Natchez Villages

The houses of the Natchez were grander than those of neighbouring tribes. Built as great rectangles, they used bent tree saplings to provide a curving roof, reminiscent of the Conestogas and prairie schooners used by Americans in later centuries. The roofs were covered with grasses, creating a thatched look. The walls consisted of pliable reeds and sticks, which were woven horizontally through wooden poles set in the ground. When this great basket of a house was completed, the people covered the framework with mud, that was then whitewashed over, creating homes that were cool in summer and snug in the mild winters of the Southeast. Such dwellings were dark because no windows were included. A fire burned constantly inside and was used for cooking and heat. Since the Natchez generally did not include a smoke hole in the roof of their houses, an ashen cloud generally hovered about the house, escaping through the door. Often the Natchez surrounded their villages with fortifications, which included wooden perimeter fencing. Such villages frequently also had a great community house and a temple that dominated the scene.

The Chief of the Natchez

While nearly all North American Indian tribes boasted a ruling structure that was dominated by chiefs, the Natchez system was an extraordinary one in this regard. As already noted, the people of the tribe referred to their leader as the 'Great Sun'. He symbolized a divine leader on earth who received complete deference from those he ruled as the head of the Natchez Sun clan. To them, he was a god. Eight men of the tribe carried the Great Sun in a sedan chair of sorts. At his approach, all bowed. No one was to ever turn his or her back to the Great Sun. He was installed at the top of one of the Natchez mounds, from

where he served as the tribe's religious and political leader. His lodge was built on top of a mound. His dwelling place was off limits to commoners, the so-called Stinkards, and could be entered only by a handful of tribal elders and the chief's wives, known as the 'Honoured People', which made up the tribal aristocracy. Yet so important was the chief himself that, when a Great Sun died, his wife and closest associates were executed, allowing them to continue serving their great ruler in the afterlife.

A visiting French explorer, a Jesuit priest named Pierre Charlevoix who had contact with the Natchez in the 1720s, presents an eyewitness account of the Great Sun at work:

> Every morning as soon as the Sun appears, the great chief comes to the door of his cabin, turns himself to the east, and howls three times, bowing down to the earth. Then they bring him a calumet [smoking pipe], which serves only for this purpose. He smokes, and blows the smoke of his tobacco towards the Sun; then he does the same thing towards the other three parts of the world. He acknowledges no superior but the Sun, from which he pretends to derive his origin. He exercises an unlimited power over his subjects, can dispose of their goods and lives, and for whatever labours he requires of them they cannot demand any recompense.

This tight class structure was rounded out by the Great Sun's kin, known as Little Suns. Dominant among them was the chief's next youngest brother. Military leaders for the Natchez came from this clan. The women of the Sun clan also carried a relative weight, for they had the power and responsibility to appoint new chiefs when Great Suns died.

The Great Sun exerted a theocratic control over his people, so much so that even in death, the Natchez continued to sacrifice on behalf of their ruler-god. When a Great Sun died, an elaborate ceremony followed, resulting in the deaths of those closest to him. During elaborate funerary rites, the Great Sun's wives, servants and lodging guards were killed so they could accompany him to the afterworld. Others could volunteer to die as well if they wished to follow their leader in his next life. During a prescribed ritual, generally taking place four days after the Great Sun's death, those marked for death ate a tobacco-based mixture, which caused them to pass out. Once unconscious, family members strangled them to death. All the fires of the Natchez village were extinguished. Another was set, as the villagers burned the Great Sun's lodge to the ground. Then their chief's body was buried. However, months later, village priests dug up his bones and placed them in a sacred basket, which was then housed in the tribal temple. During this ceremony, the men guarding the temple were also executed, so they could protect their royal leader in his new, spiritual domain.

The mound-building culture of the Natchez did not survive the arrival of Europeans in North America. By the 1720s, relations with French traders had deteriorated into war and acts of retaliation. Through an alliance of the French and the Choctaws, neighbours of the Natchez, the mound-builders were defeated. Most were killed and a few hundred were shipped down the Mississippi, where they were eventually sold into slavery in the French West Indies. A lucky few fled and were later absorbed into the tribes of the Creek, Cherokee and Chickasaw Indians.

With the elimination of the Natchez people, other tribes of the Southeast rose in significance. The Natchez were the last of the mound-building societies of ancient America. While other tribes – including the Chickasaws, Choctaws and Cherokees – were still building mounds in the 1700s, these cultures were in a state of change and flux, which eventually resulted in their abandonment of mound-building.

The Five Nations

In time, the arrival of Europeans to the Southeast spelled disaster for all the tribes of Native Americans. The Natchez were not even the first victims of European contact, as Floridan tribes including the Apalachees Calusas and Timucuas had been destroyed by the Spanish in earlier years. Several tribes did retain dominant power in the Southeast, however, until the nineteenth century. Among them and foremost were those tribal groups which banded together to form the confederacy known as the Five Civilized Tribes. This

union included the Cherokees, Chickasaws, Choctaws, Creeks and the group known as the Isty-Semole, a mixed group of refugee Creeks and escaped slaves who, by the middle of the 1700s, had found one another in the swamps of Florida, creating a tribe known for their hunting abilities and a lack of agriculture. The Isty-Semole, a name given them by the Northern Creeks meaning 'wild men', became known as the Seminoles, which translates as 'runaways'.

As these tribes took on the culture and ways of whites, their life patterns altered dramatically. By the 1820s and 1830s, the Five Civilized Tribes were not only practising the white man's agriculture, with modern tools and equipment, but were also building Anglo-American houses, using skills and crafts including blacksmithing, and dressing in the fashions of white culture. One Cherokee leader, named Sequoyah, even invented a Cherokee alphabet, which led to the publishing of a tribal newspaper, the writing of a Cherokee constitution of government (which mirrored the US Constitution) and well-delineated legal codes to be followed by all members of the tribe.

However, despite the assimilation of white culture and practices by these tribes, this did not save the tribes from tragedy at the hands of whites. Throughout the 1820s and 1830s, the United States government forced the removal of each of the five tribes from their homelands in Alabama, Georgia, Mississippi, Tennessee and Florida to reservation lands west of the Mississippi River. These forced marches, at the direct hands of US Army soldiers, are a dark chapter in United States – Native American relations. The results were the irretrievable disruption of new ways of life for the tribes and also fragmentation of their ancient heritage.

Warfare Among the Southeastern Tribes

As with nearly all the tribes of North America, the Indians of the Southeast were constantly in conflict with one another. Warring was considered necessary as a gauge of one's prowess as a male member of the tribe. Southeastern peoples developed a standing arsenal of both offensive and defensive weapons and tactics. Among those weapons that were common among Southeastern tribes were the ubiquitous bow and arrow, as well as a wide variety of war clubs, darts, scalping knives, tomahawks and shields. After extensive contact and trade with Europeans, these tribes had also gained access to the gun. The erection of wooden fences or palisades ringing the perimeter of an encampment helped to protect a village from raids by a fractious enemy. At the gate or entrance of such a palisade, a tribe often placed a pair of guards. Anyone not doing his duty as a watchman might receive a beating from other warriors wielding heavy clubs.

In preparation for battle, many Southeastern tribal warriors went through an elaborate process of rituals. In some tribes, once war had been decided on, a war leader danced three times around his lodge to the beat of a war drum. All members of the tribe who wanted to join in the fight then expressed their interest. (Rarely did all the warriors of a given tribe participate in the same warring party; frequently more than one raiding party at a time might be following the 'warrior's path'. Once the party was formed, warriors prepared their weapons and gathered food for their expedition. A ritual fast was observed and warriors went through a litany of ceremonies to prepare themselves and to receive blessings from above. Warriors commonly slathered bear grease on their hair, while the women of the tribe decorated the men's bodies and faces with paint, feathers, beadwork and copper ornaments. Generally, swan's feathers were given to a tribe's ordinary warriors, while war leaders were adorned with eagle's feathers. A war dance was held, which might stretch on for two or three days, followed by a great feast for the warriors, while their relatives fasted. Most veteran war leaders began their march at daybreak, the warriors sending musket volleys into the air, followed closely by great war whoops.

Once on their way, the warrior band remained silent at all times while following the forest paths. Certain taboos and superstitions marked their time. For example, warriors were not to lean against trees and, if they sat, were to squat on rocks. Any warrior who experienced a bad dream might be sent back to the tribe's village, as such visions were considered omens.

Even the sounds of certain birds in the woods might be enough to indicate doom for the war party and the entire effort might be completely abandoned.

A warrior wore little into combat. Among the Creek and Chickasaw tribes, for example, a warrior wore a breechclout, a belt and moccasins. After having his face painted red and black, he and his group set out for combat. Such warriors typically carried with them a blanket, leather strips and cords for repairing clothing and moccasins, and some dried corn in a leather bag for a quick meal, literally, on the run. Weapons might include a bow and arrows, a knife, a tomahawk, a war club and a spear. By the early 1700s, such warriors might carry a musket or rifle acquired through trade with European merchants, or even a flintlock pistol or two.

Warriors sometimes went to great lengths to engage an enemy. A British observer, noting Southeastern war practices in the early eighteenth century, describes a common form of Indian raid:

A body of Indians will travel four or five hundred miles to surprise a town of their enemies, travelling by night only, for some days before they approach the town. Their usual time of attack is at break of day, when, if they are not discovered, they fall on [the town] with dreadful slaughter, and scalping, which is to cut off the skins of the crown of the temples, and taking the whole head of hair along with it as if it was a night cap: sometimes they take the top of the scull with it; all which they preserve, and carefully keep by them for a trophy of their conquest. Their caution and temerity is such, that at the least noise, or suspicion of being discovered, though at the point of execution, they will give over the attack, and retreat back again with precipitation.

Southeastern warriors made no hesitation about scalping not only male members of an enemy's tribe but the women and children as well. Less honour was attached to the latter, however. Once an enemy was defeated, a ritual followed. After killing an enemy, warriors marked signs on nearby trees as a testimonial of the murderous event. Once scalped, the body was frequently carved up, with some of the parts being carried by victorious braves back to their village.

The activity of scalping increased a warrior's status with his people. Any captives taken during an engagement were often returned to the victor's camp, where the women of the tribe paid in tobacco for the privilege of whipping the prisoners. Typically, prisoners were forced to perform for the tribe, singing and dancing for days on end until they were presented to the relatives of warriors who had been killed by their enemy. Female captives had their hair cut off and were often kept as slaves for life. Males were subjected to a horrific trial which included many blows from war clubs and a scalping. Then they were fastened to a square of thick branches, a fire was set under them and they were burned to death, sacrificed on behalf of the victorious tribe.

Southeastern Indian Mythology

The mythology of the Southeastern tribes is a rich heritage of stories, tales and legends. As the Natchez tribe was an early casualty of European contact, their myths reach the modern reader in a form that was probably corrupted and distorted by many subsequent transformations. The same may be said of the legends of other Southeastern tribes, including the Creeks. Although the Creeks' culture survived white contact, the result was often a combining of ancient Creek stories with European stories, as well as with African-American tales introduced by black slaves. For example, the Creeks' stories of the trickster rabbit bear an uncanny resemblance to the tales that the Southern writer Joel Chandler Harris wrote in his famous *Uncle Remus* stories, which included such whimsical characters as Brer Rabbit, Brer Fox and Brer Wolf.

Many of the tales of the Southeast bring human beings into direct contact with nature and the animal world. This is, of course, a tendency in much of the Native American literature. For example, for a warrior male to practise his skill at the hunt he needed to have at his disposal both personal courage and technical skill. These powers came from the spirit world and, more directly, from the animals themselves. Animal powers granted to hunters, generally through dreams or vision quests, provided supernatural assistance. All this is of great importance to the would-be warrior. His status in the tribe depended on his skill at the hunt. As his hunting skills improved, and this would occur only when he received an infusion of animal prowess and skill, so did his position in his tribe.

Animal spirits could not only improve gaming technique and prowess but also grant other skills to humans. Visions and dreams could give specific skills, such as curative powers. Tribal doctors and medicine men received from the animal spirits their knowledge of how to cure disease or grant immunity from an otherwise deadly contagion. These healers, therefore, were seen as spiritual leaders, since they gained their art from animals. Others might become prophets and seers of the future among the tribe. Again, the mythology reflects such a belief. Among the South-eastern tribes, simple events in nature took on great significance. Indian prophets might see significance in the howling of a dog or a wolf, or the hoot of a night owl in a distant tree.

Cosmic events, such as shooting stars, might announce troubles for the tribe, including a war or an epidemic. Among the Cherokees, when a person sneezed, it was interpreted as a sign of good luck. In several Southeastern tribes, prophets were divided into different classes, each having specific special skills. One group, called the 'Knowers', was considered capable of predicting the future. Often twin brothers were likely candidates for becoming such prophets. The famous nineteenth-century Shawnee chief Tecumseh had a twin brother, Tenskatawa, who was known throughout the Southeast as the Prophet.

Cosmogonic Tales

Woven into the tapestry of Indian legends are tales considered to be cosmogonic in nature. These are designed to explain where something originated from or how it came into being. They seek to answer common, almost mundane questions, such as where strawberries, fish or pine trees come from, as well as more cosmic concerns, including the origins of the Milky Way galaxy, the heavenly bodies, the earth, disease and the existence of evil and sin.

Such stories often interweave simple and complex plot lines. Naturally, to the modern, scientifically minded reader, many seem naïve. For example, a Cherokee story seeks to explain how man received the use of fire. The Thunders had original control of fire and kept it in a hollow sycamore tree. After many failed attempts to recover it were made by various animals of the forests, it was finally stolen by a lowly water spider, who carried a live coal on its back in a web-woven bowl. In such stories, often a small creature is presented as a heroic figure. Other tales explain how disease was created by the animal kingdom as a way of combating man.

Sometimes the legends explained the cosmic in the simplest terms. Meteors hurtling across the night sky might be interpreted as snakes or lions on their way to new worlds. Eclipses might be explained as the work of giant toads eating away at the sun or the moon. Rainbows were, to the Southeastern story-teller, great serpents whose arched bands cut off rainfall from the earth.

Southeastern Indian Deities and Animal Spirits

As with all native cultures, the Southeastern Indians recognized a pantheon of gods and goddesses. Serving as the supreme deity for the Creeks was a being known as Hisagita-imisi, which translates as 'The Preserver of Breath'. Such a god was directly associated with the sun. On earth, he was represented by a fire spirit. Other spirits existed on earth, including the four winds, thunder and lightning. Spirits were found in animals and plants and their powers were, as has been previously mentioned, transferable to

human beings. Various varieties of snake were greatly honoured by Southeastern tribes, and other animals were accorded similar prestige. Eagles and hawks were highly regarded. Owls, and one variety of red-headed woodpecker, were known for their powers to see the future.

Southeastern Religion

Although there were many variations between the Southeastern tribes, their religion shared many of the same roots. Both the Chickasaws and the Creeks recognized a supreme being who lived above the earth in the Sky World and effected connection between the two spheres. The spirits of deceased human beings could experience an afterlife. Their souls were thought to be wanderers and travellers, always moving west, where the sun died each day. Souls considered worthy found their way to the Sky World, where they could reside with the supreme beings. Evil individuals were doomed to wander in the west for ever, where witches and ghosts dwelled.

According to Creek and Chickasaw beliefs, all humans had two souls. It was the inner soul, called the *shilup* or 'inside shadow', that spirited its way to the afterlife. Some received comfort, while others, such as those who committed murder, were relegated to a hellish place. To provide for the journey to the afterlife, Southeastern tribes buried their dead with food, clothing and the weapons and tools necessary to complete the trip. The alternate soul, known as the *shilombish* or 'outside shadow', remained on earth, taking the form of a ghost. Such a spirit could take on animal form, disguising itself as an owl, fox or other creature of the forest.

MYTHS AND LEGENDS
OF THE SOUTHEAST

THE CEDAR TREE
Yuchi

AN UNKNOWN MYSTERIOUS BEING once came down upon the earth and met people there who were the ancestors of the Yuchi Indians. To them this being taught many of the arts of life, and in matters of religion admonished them to call the sun their mother as a matter of worship. Every morning the sun, after rising above the horizon, makes short stops, and then goes faster until it reaches the noon point. So the Unknown inquired of them what was the matter with the sun. They denied having any knowledge about it, and said, 'Somebody has to go there to see and examine it.' 'Who would go there, and what could he do after he gets there?' The people said, 'We are afraid to go up there.' But the Unknown selected two men to make the ascent, gave to each a club, and instructed them that as soon as the wizard who was playing these tricks on the sun was leaving his cavern in the earth and appeared on the surface, they should kill him on the spot. 'It is a wizard who causes the sun to go so fast in the morning, for at sunrise he makes dashes at it, and the sun, being afraid of him, tries to flee from his presence.'

The two brave men went to the rising place of the sun to watch the orifice from which the sun emerges. The wizard appeared at the mouth of the cave, and at the same time the sun was to rise from another orifice beyond it. The Wizard watched for the fiery disc and put himself in position to rush and jump at it at the moment of its appearance. When the wizard held up his head, the two men knocked it off from his body with their clubs, took it to their tribe and proclaimed that they had killed the sorcerer who had for so long a time urged the sun to a quicker motion. But the wizard's head was not dead yet. It was stirring and moving about, and to stop this the man of mysterious origin advised the people to tie the head on the uppermost limbs of a tree. They did so, and on the next morning the head fell to the ground, for it was not dead yet. He then ordered them to tie the head to another tree. It still lived and fell to the ground the next day. To ensure success, the Unknown then made them tie it to a red cedar tree. There it remained, and its life became extinct. The blood of the head ran through the cedar. Henceforth the grain of the wood assumed a reddish colour, and the cedar tree became a medicine tree.

Source
Albert S. Gatschet. 'Some Mythic Stories of the Yuchi Indians', *American Anthropologist* (OS), 6 (1893), pp. 279–82

ADOPTION OF THE HUMAN RACE

Natchez

IN THE VERY BEGINNING, Moon, Sun, Wind, Rainbow, Thunder, Fire and Water together met a very old man whom they later discovered was the Chief of the Sky Spirits. Thunder asked him, 'Can you make the human beings of the world children of mine?' 'No, never,' said the Wise Old One. 'The human beings may not be your children, but they may become your grandchildren.' 'Can you make the human beings of the world children of mine?' asked the Sun. 'No, they may not be children of yours,' replied the Old One. 'They may, however, become your friends and your grandchildren. They may receive much light from you.' Moon asked of the Old Man, 'Can you make the human beings of the world children of mine?' 'No, I may not do such a thing,' said the Old One. 'They may be your nephews and friends.' Fire then took his turn and asked, 'Can you make the human beings of the world children of mine?' The Wise Old One gave his reply: 'No, I may not make them your children, but they may be your grandchildren, also. It will be your purpose to give them warmth and heat to cook their food.' Wind asked the same question: 'Can you make the human beings of the world children of mine?' And again the Wise Old One answered, 'No, they may not be made your children, but, as I have told the others, they may become your grandchildren. You will keep them healthy by blowing away the foul air and with it the diseases which make the human beings sick.' The rainbow asked as well and the Old One told him, 'They may not be your children, but you will be there for them to clean themselves when they are soiled and dirty. By doing so, you will give them long life.'

After telling them each these things, the Wise Old One reminded each of them, 'I have given you instructions concerning how each of you may give help and comfort to the human beings of the world. And ever must you remember that the children of earth – the human race – are my children.'

'And ever must you remember that the children of earth – the human race – are my children' said the Wise Old One.

Source
John R. Swanton, 'Adoption of the Human Race', *BAE Bulletin*, 42 (1924–5), p. 240

HOW RABBIT FOOLED ALLIGATOR

Creek

LONG AGO, when the animals could talk as human beings do today, an alligator of extraordinary good looks lay in the warm sun on a log in the everglades. Mr Rabbit soon came hopping along and addressed the alligator: 'Have you ever seen the devil, Mr Handsome Alligator?' 'No,' said Mr Alligator. 'I have not seen the devil, but if I did, I would not fear him.' 'Well, I have seen the devil,' said Mr Rabbit. 'And he spoke of you.' The Alligator then asked, 'Well, what did the devil have to say?' 'The devil was certain that you feared him so much you would not even look at him.'

The Alligator assured the Rabbit that he was not afraid of the devil and he asked Mr Rabbit to give that message to him next time he saw him. The Rabbit replied, 'The day after tomorrow, you could crawl up the hill and tell him yourself, Mr Alligator. But I don't think you will be willing to make the trip.' 'But I

Source
John R. Swanton, 'How Rabbit Fooled Alligator', *BAE Bulletin*, 88 (1929), pp. 115–16

will,' said the Alligator. 'In fact, let's go tomorrow rather than wait.' 'Fine,' said Mr Rabbit. 'Now you should know that when you climb the hill tomorrow, if you see smoke, don't worry. That just means that the devil is on his way to meet you.' 'I will be prepared to meet him,' said Mr Alligator. 'And if you witness deer galloping past you and birds flying swiftly past, don't worry.' The Alligator continued to assure Mr Rabbit that he would not worry and was not afraid of meeting the devil. The Rabbit continued, 'If you hear the crackle of fire nearby and if the grass around you smokes and burns, do not be afraid, for it will only be the devil walking nearby. In fact, when the heat is intense around you, that is the best time to see the devil.' Finally, Mr Rabbit left Mr Alligator, who continued sunning himself on his log.

The next day, Mr Rabbit returned and began encouraging Mr Alligator to begin his crawl up the hill, assuring him that he would be close behind him. Once they reached the top, Rabbit instructed Alligator to wait in the tall grass on the hill. Soon, Alligator was alone as Rabbit scampered away. As Rabbit hopped down the hill, he laughed and laughed. He knew Alligator was now a great distance from his home in the swamp.

On his way down the hill, Rabbit came upon a low burning tree stump. Rabbit picked up some coals and carried them back up the hill, setting the tall grass on fire with Mr Alligator nearby. Soon a fire was burning through the tall grass, coming closer and closer to Mr Alligator. Rabbit moved out of the tall grass to a sandy spot where he could watch the fire and talk to the Alligator.

Soon the smoke from the fire was thick across the hill top. Birds flew away and the forest animals began to stampede away and down the hill. Rabbit could hear Alligator call his name: 'Mr Rabbit, are you there?' Rabbit reassured him: 'Do not be afraid, Mr Alligator, it is only the devil drawing near.' As the fire grew and became quite hot, Alligator again called out to Rabbit, 'What is that noise I hear, Mr Rabbit?' 'It is the devil's breath,' said Rabbit. 'Just remain where you are, and do not be afraid. The devil is very near you.'

Then the fire began to burn the grass near Alligator. As Rabbit watched, he was rolling around in laughter. Soon, the fire was burning Alligator and he writhed in pain at the heat and flames. Rabbit continued to encourage Alligator to remain calm and not to move. 'The devil is very close now, Mr Alligator. You must not be afraid or you will miss your opportunity to see him face to face.'

But Alligator could not wait any longer. He began crawling out of the burning grass and down the hill towards his swamp. He was covered with burns and was choking on the smoke of the fire. Meanwhile, Rabbit continued laughing at the trick he had played on Alligator. He called out to him, 'Wait, Mr Alligator, wait. If you leave now, you will miss seeing the devil. You must be afraid of him, after all.' When he reached the bottom of the hill, Alligator slipped into the swampy water, his skin charred and roasted. No longer was he a handsome alligator. He had been tricked by Rabbit and he was always careful after that never to trust Mr Rabbit again or even any member of the Rabbit's family.

INCEST OF THE SUN AND MOON

Cherokee

THE SUN WAS A YOUNG WOMAN and lived in the east, while her brother, the Moon, lived in the west. The girl had a lover who used to come every month in the dark of the Moon to court her. He would come at night, and leave before daylight, and although she talked with him she could not see his face in the dark, and he would not tell her his name, until she was wondering all the time who it could be. At last she hit upon a plan to find out, so the next time he came, as they were sitting together in the dark of the *asi* (wigwam), she slyly dipped her hand into the cinders and ashes of the fireplace and rubbed it over his face, saying, 'Your face is cold; you must have suffered from the wind,' and pretending to be very sorry for him, but he did not know that she had ashes on her hand. After a while he left her and went away again.

The next night when the Moon came up in the sky his face was covered with spots, and then his sister knew he was the one who had been coming to see her. He was so much ashamed to have her know it that he kept as far away as he could at the other end of the sky all the night. Ever since he tries to keep a long way behind the Sun, and when he does sometimes have to come near her in the west he makes himself as thin as a ribbon so that he can hardly be seen.

Source
James Mooney, 'Myths of the Cherokees', *BAEAR*, 19:2 (1900), pp. 256–7

THE THEFT OF FIRE

Cherokee

IN THE BEGINNING there was no fire and the world was cold, until the Thunders (Ani'-Hyun'tikwala'ski), who lived up in Galun'lati, sent their lightning and put fire into the bottom of a hollow sycamore tree which grew on an island. The animals knew it was there, because they could see the smoke coming out at the top, but they could not get to it on account of the water, so they held a council to decide what to do. This was a long time ago.

Every animal that could fly or swim was anxious to go after the fire. The Raven offered, and because he was so large and strong they thought he could surely do the work, so he was sent first. He flew high and far across the water and alighted on the sycamore tree, but while he was wondering what to do next, the heat had scorched all his feathers black, and he was frightened and came back without the fire. The little Screech Owl (Wa'huhu') volunteered to go, and reached the place safely, but while he was looking down into the hollow tree a blast of hot air came up and nearly burned out his eyes. He managed to fly home as best he could, but it was a long time before he could see well, and his eyes are red to this day. Then the Hooting Owl (U'guku) and the Horned Owl (Tskili') went, but by the time they got to the hollow tree the fire was burning so fiercely that the smoke nearly blinded them, and the ashes carried up by the wind made white rings about their eyes. They had to come home again without the fire, but with all their rubbing they were never able to get rid of the white rings.

Now no more of the birds would venture, and so the little Uksu'hi snake, the

Source
James Mooney, 'Myths of the Cherokees', *BAEAR*, 19: 2 (1900), pp. 240–1

black racer, said he would go through the water and bring back some fire. He swam across to the island and crawled through the grass to the tree, and went in by a small hole at the bottom. The heat and smoke were too much for him, too, and after dodging about blindly over the hot ashes until he was almost on fire himself, he managed by good luck to get out again at the same hole, but his body had been scorched black, and he has ever since had the habit of darting and doubling on his track as if trying to escape from close quarters. He came back, and the great blacksnake, Gule'gi (the Climber), offered to go for fire. He swam over to the island and climbed up the tree on the outside, as the blacksnake always does, but when he put his head down into the hole the smoke choked him so that he fell into the burning stump, and before he could climb out again he was as black as the Uksu'hi.

Now they held another council, for still there was no fire and the world was cold, but birds, snakes and four-footed animals, all had some excuse for not going, because they were all afraid to venture near the burning sycamore, until at last Kanane'ski Amai'yehi (the Water Spider) said she would go. This is not the water spider that looks like a mosquito, but the other one, with black downy hair and red stripes on her body. She can run on top of the water or dive to the bottom, so there would be no trouble to get over to the island, but the question was, How could she bring back the fire?

'I'll manage that,' said the Water Spider. So she spun a thread from her body and wove it into a little bowl, which she fastened on her back. Then she crossed over to the island and through the grass to where the fire was still burning. She put one little coal of fire into her bowl and came back with it, and ever since we have had fire, and the Water Spider still keeps her *tusti* bowl.

THE ORIGIN OF ANIMALS (CLANS)

Tuskegee and Creek

THE OLD-TIME BEINGS were gathered together. They began acting in different ways and showing different qualities. Master of Breath observed them. Some began jumping upon trees and running about. Someone asked, 'What sort of beings are those?'

The origin of animals (clans).

'They are like panthers,' someone answered.

'Henceforth they shall go about as panthers,' said Master of Breath. Then again, some began leaping and running.

'What are they like?' someone asked.

Source
Frank G. Speck,
'The Creek
Indians of
Taskigi Town',
*American
Anthropological
Society Memoirs*,
2, 2 (1907),
pp. 146ff

'Like deer,' it was said.

'Henceforth they shall go about as deer,' said Master of Breath. Then again, some went hopping high among the leaves of trees and alighted on the branches.

'What are they like?' asked somebody.

'Like birds,' someone answered.

'They shall be birds,' said Master of Breath. Then again, some were very fat and when they walked they made a great noise on the ground.

'What are they like?' asked someone.

'Like bears,' was the answer.

'They shall be bears, then,' said Master of Breath. Then again, one started off to run but could not go fast. When he came back he had black stripes near his eyes.

'What will that be?' it was asked.

'It is like a racoon,' said one.

'That kind shall be racoons,' said Master of Breath. Then one was so fat and round-bodied that when he started off he could hardly walk.

'What is that kind?' it was asked.

'It is like a beaver,' someone answered.

'They shall be the beavers,' said Master of Breath. Then again, one kind was fat and could not run very fast. When this one had gone off to a distance and returned, someone asked, 'What is that like?'

'Like a mink.'

'They shall go about as minks,' said Master of Breath. Then again, one was very swift when he started to run. He darted back and forth very quickly.

'What is he like?' was the question.

'Like a fox,' came the answer.

'That kind shall be foxes,' said Master of Breath. Then again, one was very strong and could pull up saplings by the roots. He went off to a distance and returned. Then someone asked, 'What is he like?'

'Like the wind,' was the answer.

'That kind shall be wind,' said Master of Breath. Then again, one started off into the mud. When he had come back out of it, someone asked, 'What is he like?'

'Like a mud-potato,' it was answered.

'Such shall be mud-potatoes,' said Master of Breath. Then again, one of them had short legs and his back was covered with ridges. When he started out and returned, someone asked, 'What is he like?'

'Like an alligator,' was the answer.

'That kind shall be alligators,' said Master of Breath. Then again, one with stripes on his back went running off, and when he came back, someone asked, 'What is he like?'

'Like a skunk,' was the answer.

'That kind shall be skunks,' said Master of Breath. Then again, one went away jumping, and when he came back to the starting place, someone asked, 'What is he like?'

'Like a rabbit,' was the answer.

'That kind shall be rabbits,' said Master of Breath. Then again, one went off squirming along on the ground. When he returned, someone asked, 'What is he like?'

'Like a snake,' was the answer.

'That kind shall be snakes,' said Master of Breath.

Master of Breath, after he had given them their forms on the earth, told them not to marry their own kind, but to marry people of other clans. All the red people know what clans they belong to and do not marry in their own clan. If they did they would not increase.

THE ORIGIN OF EARTH
Tuskegee

BEFORE THE BEGINNING, water was to be found everywhere. Only water was visible and there were no human beings, animals or even the earth to be seen. Only the birds were in existence and they flew above the water.

One day the birds held a council to decide whether they should remain where only the water existed or seek out land. Some of the birds wanted land so that food would be more plentiful. Others among the birds were content being surrounded by water, saying it was all they had ever known and they did not want to change. Since they could not agree among themselves, the birds appealed to the Eagle, who was to be their chief. He was to decide whether they would remain in a water world or go and seek out land.

After deciding in favour of land, the Eagle asked the birds who among them might go out and search for land. The dove volunteered first and was soon off in flight. Four days passed before his return. He told the other birds, 'I flew for four days and could find no land anywhere.'

At that moment, Crawfish swam near the bird council and they asked him if he was willing to help the birds find land.

Agreeing, Crawfish swam beneath the water, only to return after four days had passed. With his return, he held in his claws some soil, which he showed to the birds. He said he had discovered land far beneath the waters. He took the dirt and formed it into the shape of a ball. He gave it to Chief Eagle and the Chief flew off with the ball of dirt.

Four days later, Chief Eagle returned and announced to the bird council that he had created an island with the ball of soil. 'Follow me,' he told the birds. All the birds followed after Chief Eagle until they arrived near a small island. As they watched, the little island began to grow ever bigger. As the land grew, the waters began to recede, until the island grew even more. Other islands appeared, some connecting to one another. The larger islands slowly formed into one earth.

Once the earth had been formed, the Great Spirit placed the Tuskegee people on it first as the earth's first human beings. All this happened a long, long time ago.

Source
John R. Swanton, 'Creation', *BAE Bulletin*, 42 (1924–5), p. 487

EARTH-DIVER
Creek and Yuchi

THE TIME WAS, in the beginning, when the earth overflowed with water. There was no earth, no beast of the earth, no human being. They held a council to know which would be best, to have some land or to have all water. When the council had met, some said, 'Let us have land, so that we can get food,' because they would starve to death. But others said, 'Let us have all water,' because they wanted it that way.

So they appointed Eagle as chief. He was told to decide one way or another. Then he decided. He decided for land. So they looked around for someone whom they could send out to get land. The first one to propose himself was Dove, who thought that he could do it. Accordingly they sent him. He was given four days in

Source
Frank G. Speck, 'The Creek Indians of Taskigi Town', *American Anthropological Society Memoirs*, 2, 2 (1907), pp. 145–7

which to perform his task. Now when Dove came back on the fourth day, he said that he could find no land. They concluded to try another plan. Then they obtained the services of Crawfish (Sakdju). He went down through the water into the ground beneath and he too was gone four days. On the fourth morning he arose and appeared on the surface of the waters. In his claws they saw that he held some dirt. He had at last secured the land. Then they took the earth from his claws and made a ball of it. When this was completed they handed it over to the chief, Eagle, who took it and went out from their presence with it. When he came back to the council, he told them that there was land, an island. So all the beasts went in the direction pointed out and found that there was land there, as Eagle had said. But what they found was very small. They lived there until the water receded from this earth. Then the land all joined into one.

THE HERO WITH THE HORNED SNAKE

Cherokee

LONG AGO, MAGIC SNAKES lived on the earth. They were giant snakes with a skin which shone brightly in the sun. Each snake had two horns and carried great power. It was considered a bad sign when one even saw one of these snakes. When anyone ran from one of these snakes, the snake used its magic to lure its victim to it and would then eat it. Killing such a creature was nearly impossible. Only a shaman or hunter who possessed great skill and cunning could kill any of these dreadful two-horned snakes. Such hunters could kill the beast only by shooting an arrow into its skin, piercing the snake's seventh stripe.

One day the Cherokees captured a young Shawnee brave. To gain his freedom, the Shawnee lad agreed to hunt down and kill one of the two-horned snakes. The young warrior hunted across the land, searching in dark caves and over the rugged Tennessee Mountains, until he found one. Immediately, the youth prepared to make the kill. He built a fire circle by burning pine cones. Approaching the snake, the Shawnee brave fired an arrow into the monster, shouting, 'Freedom or death!' The arrow struck the seventh stripe. Then the youth jumped into the ring of fire where he would be safe from the snake. When venom flowed out of the snake, it streamed towards the young Shawnee, but the fire circle stopped its advance. Because he had committed this act of bravery, the Cherokees freed their Shawnee captive, as they had promised.

Several days later, some Cherokee warriors went to the site where the Shawnee lad had killed a two-horned snake. They collected the snake's remains, including the bones and skin, placing them inside a sacred bundle. These things they kept in the bundle as a source of good fortune for the future of the tribe, for their children and grandchildren.

When venom flowed out of the snake, it streamed towards the young Shawnee, but the fire circle stopped its advance.

Source

H. Kate, 'The Hero with the Horned Snake', *JAFL*, 2 (1889), p. 55

THE WALNUT-CRACKER

Creek

MANY, MANY YEARS AGO in western Georgia, there lived a Southeastern Creek-Hitchiti Indian named Walnut-cracker. Members of his tribe named him this because he spent many of his days at one place collecting, cracking and eating walnuts. He would crack the walnuts with a small stone. Every day, even into the evenings, Walnut-cracker sat and ate walnuts. For years, this activity was all Walnut-cracker did until his death. When he died, the men of his tribe buried his body near the spot where Walnut-cracker had cracked and eaten his walnuts all those years.

One day, some time after the death of Walnut-cracker, a Creek brave was passing through the forest, near the spot where Walnut-cracker had laboured and died. There he discovered a large mound of walnuts and, as he was hungry, he sat himself down and cracked open several walnuts, eating the tasty nut meat. Later that same day, the Creek hunter returned and cracked open even more walnuts, eating them as well. While he sat and worked at Walnut-cracker's old spot, another Creek warrior happened to walk by and heard the sound of someone cracking walnuts. He approached and, peering through the evening darkness, thought he saw Walnut-cracker once more at his work.

Bewildered and surprised, the warrior ran back to his village and told the people that he had seen Walnut-cracker cracking walnuts once again at his old haunt. The man asked his people, 'Could Walnut-cracker's ghost be at work?' The Creek warrior's family all decided to visit the place where Walnut-cracker had lived. Were they surprised when they, too, saw someone squatting among the rocks, cracking walnuts? They, also, thought the man they saw was Walnut-cracker.

One member of the Creek warrior's family had been a good friend of Walnut-cracker. He was a lame man and asked his clansmen to carry him to the spot where Walnut-cracker's 'ghost' had been spotted. 'Carry me on your back,' he asked. 'I must see if the one you have seen is my friend Walnut-cracker.'

So Lame Man was carried to the spot and he saw through the darkness a figure sitting cracking walnuts. 'Take me closer,' said Lame Man, and his bearer carried him closer. The hunter could not hear the men approaching since he was busy cracking walnuts. Still Lame Man told his carrier, 'Take me even closer, so I may see him.'

When Lame Man came very close to the mysterious figure, the hunter heard him approach and leapt up, taking his bow and arrows, running away. In surprise and fear, when the hunter leapt up and ran, so did those watching him. In fear, Lame Man's bearer dropped him and ran back to his village. Frightened, Lame Man jumped to his feet and ran to catch up with his people. It appeared that his fear had cured him of his lameness. In fact, he ran so fast that he outran everyone else, arriving back at their lodge before they arrived. After this frightful encounter, Lame Man was able to walk for the rest of his days.

As for Walnut-cracker, his 'ghost' was never seen again.

'Could Walnut-cracker's Ghost still be at work?'

Source
John R. Swanton, 'The Walnut-cracker', *BAE Bulletin*, 88 (1929), pp. 115–16

JOURNEY TO THE UNDERWATER LODGE

Creek

A CHIEF SENT HIS SON with a message to another chief, and delivered to him a vessel as the emblem of his authority.

The son stopped to play with some boys who were throwing stones into the water. The chief's son threw his vessel upon the water and it sank. He was frightened. He was afraid to go to the neighbouring chief without the vessel, and he did not like to return home and tell his father of the loss. He jumped into the stream and, reaching the spot where the vessel had sunk, he dived into the water. His playmates waited a long time for him, but he did not reappear. They returned and reported his death.

When the chief's son was beneath the surface of the stream the Tie-snakes seized him and bore him to a cave and said to him, 'Ascend yonder platform.' He looked and saw seated on the platform the king of the Tie-snakes. The platform was a mass of living Tie-snakes. He approached the platform and lifted his foot to ascend, but the platform ascended as he lifted his foot. Again he tried, with the same result. The third time he tried in vain. The Tie-snakes said, 'Ascend.'

He lifted his foot the fourth time and succeeded in ascending the platform and the king invited him to sit by his side. Then the king said to him, 'See yonder feather; it is yours,' pointing to a plume in the corner of the cave. He approached the plume and extended his hand to seize it, but it eluded his grasp. Three times he made the attempt and three times it escaped him. On the fourth attempt he obtained it.

'Yonder tomahawk is yours,' said the Tie-snakes' king.

He went to the place where the tomahawk was sticking and reached out his hand to take it, but in vain. It rose of itself every time he raised his hand. He tried four times and on the fourth trial it remained still and he succeeded in taking it.

The king said, 'You can return to your father after three days. When he asks where you have been, reply, "I know what I know," but on no account tell him what you do know. When he needs my aid walk towards the east and bow three times to the rising sun and I will be there to help him.'

After three days the Tie-snake carried him to the spot where he had dived into the stream, lifted him to the surface of the water and placed his lost vessel in his hand. He swam to the bank and returned to his father, who was mourning him as dead. His father rejoiced over his son's wonderful restoration.

Source
John R.
Swanton,
'Myths and
Tales of the
Southeastern
Indians', *BAE
Bulletin*, 88
(1929),
pp. 34–5

He informed his father of the Tie-snake king and his message of proffered aid. Not long afterwards his father was attacked by his enemies. He said to his son, 'You understand what the king of the Tie-snakes said. Go and seek his aid.'

The son put the plume on his head, took the tomahawk, went towards the east and bowed three times to the rising sun.

The king of the Tie-snakes stood before him.

'What do you wish?' he said.

'My father needs your aid.'

'Go and tell him not to fear. They will attack him, but they shall not harm him or his people. In the morning all will be well.'

The son returned to his father and delivered the message of the king of the Tie-snakes.

The enemy came and attacked his town, but no one was harmed. Night came. In the morning they beheld their enemies each held fast in the folds of a Tie-snake, and so all were captured and the chief made peace with his foes.

THE BIRDS AND THE ANIMALS PLAY BALL

Cherokee

A LONG TIME AGO, the animals challenged the birds to a game of ball. 'We will defeat you,' said the animals, but the birds responded, 'We are willing to play a ball game with you and we will win.' Both animals and birds began planning for the event and a day was chosen for the game to be played.

When the animals gathered for their game, they chose the bear, the deer and the terrapin or turtle to play the ball game. The bear was chosen for his weight and size, for he was heavier than even all the birds put together. The deer was a swift runner. The terrapin was chosen for his thick shell. The animals were certain they would win the ball game. The birds were equally certain. They selected the eagle, the hawk and the raven as their players. These birds were known for their swiftness in flight. They could see great distances. Each had a sharp beak, which was strong and capable of tearing.

Before the game began, the birds were sitting in the tree tops, smoothing down their feathers, as they watched the animals on the forest floor. As they watched, two tiny creatures began climbing towards them. They were no bigger than mice. 'May we play in the game today?' they asked the chief of the birds. When the chief saw they had four legs, he asked them, 'Since you have four feet, why don't you play for the animals?' 'We wish to play on your side,' they said. 'Besides, the animals will not let us play on their side. They laughed at us when we asked them.' Feeling sorry for the tiny creatures, the bird chief asked the others if the two could play with them. The birds – including eagle and hawk – agreed.

'But how can they play on our side?' the birds asked. 'These two creatures have no wings.' Another bird answered, 'We will make wings from the skin of the drum.' The skin was that of a groundhog. The birds removed the skin and fashioned a pair of leather wings for one of the two creatures. In doing so, they created the first bat.

The chief of the birds then gave them instructions concerning the ball game. 'When I toss you the ball, you be certain to catch it and do not let it fall to the ground.' As the bat practised, he caught the ball and then flew around the trees, zigzagging as he flew. He flew very fast and in many directions. He was careful not to drop the ball. Even before the game began, the birds were glad they had made the creature his wings.

But the birds asked, 'What shall we do for the other creature? We have no more drum leather to make him a pair of wings, too.' After thinking long and hard, the birds came up with another idea. 'If we have no more skin to make him wings, let us just pull his skin until it can be made into wings.' With that, the eagle

Source
James Mooney,
'The Cherokee
Play Ball',
BAEAR, 24
(1907),
pp. 575–86

and hawk, since they were large and strong, grabbed up the little creature and began pulling on his skin with their powerful beaks. Soon, his fur between his front and hind feet was stretched out, making wings for him to fly. In this way, the birds created the first flying squirrel.

When the ball game began, the flying squirrel caught it and flew it to another tree far above the animals below. He then flew it over to the eagle. After catching it, the eagle threw it to another bird. As the game went on, the birds kept the ball away from the animals, throwing it back and forth to one another.

Finally, however, one of the birds dropped the ball. As it dropped towards the ground, the bat flew down swiftly and grabbed it! The bat continued flying, zigzagging past the animals, so that even the fast deer could not catch him. When the bat threw the ball into the goal, he had won the game for his friends, the birds.

THE MILKY WAY

Seminole

LONG, LONG AGO, the Maker of Breath blew his wind across the sky, creating the Milky Way. This path serves as the route in the sky for fallen warriors to help them find the City in the West, the place where good souls may go after an honourable death. The Seminole believe that when a Seminole soul dies, the Milky Way shines brighter to give him a clear path to the spirit world.

To walk along the path of the Milky Way, a warrior must have led a good life. It is important that he was a person whom many people liked and respected. He must not have engaged in stealing or lying or spoken evil of another. He must have been a brave individual who knew honour in his days. Once a departed soul arrives in the City in the West, he will always remain there. The Seminoles do not believe that such souls haunt the earth and come back to visit people after their deaths. When a good soul travels the Milky Way, he rides in the boat of the Big Dipper. This boat carries the souls of good Seminoles to the City in the West.

However, anyone who died whose soul was evil could not rise up into the sky, but had to remain on earth, buried in the ground. Such spirits may not escape and remain near their graves. The Seminoles have a fear of such sites and will always avoid them if possible. Seminoles seem to know when they are in the presence of such evil souls, even when their graves are obscured by bushes and undergrowth.

Along the path of the Milky Way live both Rain and Rainbow. The Seminole word for rainbow is stops-the-rain, since the rain disappears when the rainbow appears. The Seminoles believe that when the sun is in an eclipse, it is because toad-frog is moving across the sky, eating pieces of the sun until it disappears. The Seminole hunters kill toad-frogs with their arrows to help prevent such eclipses from occurring.

When a Seminole soul dies, the Milky Way shines brighter to give him a clear path to the spirit world.

Source
R.F. Greenlee, 'The Milky Way', *JAFL*, 58 (1945), pp. 138–40

THE ORIGIN OF POISON
Choctaw

LONG AGO A CERTAIN VINE grew along the edges of bayous, in shallow water. This vine was very poisonous, and often when the Choctaw would bathe or swim in the bayous they would come in contact with the vine and often become so badly poisoned that they would die as a result.

Now the vine was very kind and liked the Choctaw and consequently did not want to cause them so much trouble and pain. He would poison the people without being able to make known to them his presence there beneath the water. So he decided to rid himself of the poison. A few days later he called together the chiefs of the snakes, bees, wasps and other similar creatures and told them of his desire to give them his poison. For up to that time no snake, bee or wasp had the power it now possesses, namely that of stinging a person.

The snakes and bees and wasps, after much talk, agreed to share the poison. The rattlesnake was the first to speak and he said, 'I shall take the poison, but before I strike or poison a person I shall warn him by the noise of my tail (*intesha*); then if he does not heed me I shall strike.'

The water moccasin was the next to speak: 'I also am willing to take some of your poison; but I shall never poison a person unless he steps on me.'

The small ground rattler was the last of the snakes to speak: 'Yes, I will gladly take of your poison and I will also jump at a person whenever I have a chance.' And so it has continued to do ever since.

Source
David Bushnell, 'Myths of the Louisiana Choctaw', *American Anthropologist*, 12 (1910), pp. 526–35

MEN VISIT THE SKY TO SEE GOD
Seminole

ALONG, LONG TIME AGO, five Seminole warriors began a journey to visit the sky in hopes of seeing the Great Spirit. They walked a long distance on their trip, travelling ever to the east. After a month of walking, they reached the end of land. At the earth's edge, they tossed their belongings over and then they, too, disappeared over the rim. After falling down for some time, they began to rise upward towards the sky. They passed along the air for a long time, always towards the west. At long last, they landed near the lodge of a very old woman. She spoke to them in a feeble voice, asking, 'Tell me, for whom are you looking?' 'We are in search of the Great Spirit,' they replied. 'You may not see him now,' the Old Woman said. 'You may remain here for the time being.'

That evening the five Seminole warriors took a walk away from the Old Woman's lodge. While out walking, they came upon a group of winged, white-robed angels. These celestial men were playing a ball game similar to one the Seminoles played on earth. At this sight, two of the five Seminoles decided they would like to become angels and not return to earth. Their desire was granted when the Great Spirit appeared, saying to them, 'So be it!'

To prepare the two Seminoles for their new home, the Great Spirit placed them in a large cooking pot with a fire burning beneath it. The two men were cooked

Source
R.F. Greenlee. 'Men Visit the Sky to See God', *JAFL*, 58 (1945): p. 143

until only their bones remained. Then the Great Spirit took the bones out of the pot and put them back into their proper shape. He then placed white robes on both of them and brought them back to life with the touch of his magic stick. They had received their wish to remain and become Men-Angels. At this, the Great Spirit turned to the other three Seminoles and asked them what they wanted to do. 'With your permission, we wish to return to our earthly Seminole encampment,' they said. 'Collect your belongings and go to sleep immediately,' ordered the Great Spirit. This they did, and when they awoke, they were once again in their home village. 'We have returned,' the three warriors told their people. 'We will never journey to the sky again for we are happy to be here on earth.' These words they spoke to the chief of the Seminoles.

NANIH WAIYA

Choctaw

IN ANCIENT DAYS the ancestors of the Choctaws and the Chickasaws lived in a far western country, under the rule of two brothers, named Chahta and Chikasa. In the process of time, their population becoming very numerous, they found it difficult to procure subsistence in that land. Their prophets thereupon announced that far to the east was a country of fertile soil and full of game, where they could live in ease and plenty. The entire population resolved to make a journey eastward in search of that happy land. In order more easily to procure subsistence on their route, the people marched in several divisions of a day's journey apart. A great prophet marched at their head, bearing a pole which, on camping at the close of each day, he planted erect in earth, in front of the camp. Every morning the pole was always seen leaning in the direction they were to travel that day. After the lapse of many moons, they arrived one day at Nanih Waiya. The prophet planted his pole at the base of the mound. The next morning the pole was seen standing erect and stationary. This was interpreted as an omen from the Great Spirit that the long-sought-for land was at last found. It so happened, the very day that the party camped at Nanih Waiya, that a party under Chikasa crossed the creek and camped on its east side. That night a great rain fell, and it rained several days. In consequence of this all the low lands were inundated, and Nanih Waiya Creek and other tributaries of Pearl River were rendered impassable.

After the subsidence of the waters, messengers were sent across the creek to bid Chikasa's party to return, as the oracular pole had proclaimed that the long-sought-for land was found and the mound was the centre of the land. Chikasa's party, however, regardless of the weather, had proceeded on their journey and, the rain having washed traces of their march from off the grass, the messengers were unable to follow them up and so returned to camp. Meanwhile, the other divisions in the rear arrived at Nanih Waiya and learned that here was the centre of their new home and that their long pilgrimage was at last finished. Chikasa's party, after their separation from their brethren under Chahta, moved on to the Tombigbee, and eventually became a separate nationality. In this way the Choctaws and the Chickasaws became two separate though kindred nations.

Source

Henry S. Halbert, 'Nanih Waiya, the Sacred Mound of the Choctaws', *Publications of Mississippi Historical Society*, 2 (1899), pp. 230–33

THE MAN WHO BECAME A DEER
Choctaw

ONE NIGHT A HUNTER killed a doe and soon afterward fell asleep near the carcass. The next morning, just at sunrise, the hunter was surprised and startled to see the doe raise her head and to hear her speak, asking him to go with her to her home.

At first he was so surprised that he did not know what to reply, so the doe again asked him whether he would go. Then the hunter said that he would go with her, although he had no idea where she would lead him. So they started and the doe led the hunter through forests and over high mountains, until at last they reached a large hole under a rock, which they entered. Here the hunter was led before the king of all the deer, an immense buck, with huge antlers and a large black spot on his back.

Soon the hunter became drowsy and finally he fell asleep. Now all around the cave were piles of deer's feet, antlers and skins. While the hunter was asleep the deer endeavoured to fit to his hands and feet deer's feet which they selected for the purpose. After several unsuccessful attempts, the fourth set proved to be just the right size and were fastened firmly on the hunter's hands and feet. Then a skin was found that covered him properly, and finally antlers were fitted to his head. And then the hunter became a deer and walked on four feet after the manner of deer.

To the great astonishment of all, the deer spoke.

Many days passed, and the hunter's mother and all his friends thought he had been killed. One day when they were in the forest they found his bow and arrows hanging on a branch of the tree beneath which he had slept beside the body of the doe. All gathered around the spot and began singing, when suddenly they saw a herd of deer bounding towards them through the forest. The deer then circled about the singers. One large buck approached closer than the others and the singers, rushing forwards, caught it. To the great astonishment of all it spoke, whereupon they recognized the voice of the lost hunter.

Source
David Bushnell, 'The Choctaw of Bayou Lacomb, St Tammany Parish, LA', *BAE Bulletin*, 48 (1909), p. 32

Greatly distressed, the hunter's mother begged her companions to remove from her son the deer skin and antlers and feet, but they told her he would certainly die if they should do so. She insisted, however, saying she would rather bury her son than have him remain a deer. So her friends began tearing away the skin, which already had grown to the hunter's body, and, as they continued their efforts to remove it, the blood began to flow. Finally the hunter died. Then his body was taken back to the village where it was buried with the ceremony of a great dance.

FALSE BRIDEGROOM

Caddo

ONE TIME THERE LIVED an old man and woman who had two beautiful twin daughters. These girls heard of a chief who lived in another village, and rumours of his great wealth and his fame as a great chief had travelled far. The girls asked their parents if they might not go to the chief and offer themselves in marriage. Their parents consented, and so the girls started to the chief's village. They did not know just where the village was, but they started in the direction that they thought it was, and decided to ask the first person they met to direct them. They travelled along for a time and then met a man with a turkey in his hand coming down the road. They stopped him and began to talk to him. 'We want to marry this famous chief, for we hear that he is good and very wealthy, but we do not know him. We have never seen him, we have not even been to his village and perhaps we would not know him if we should see him.' The man grinned to himself and said, 'I am the chief and I live just a little way from here; I have been away attending a council. Well, I must say that I am willing, but wait here while I run on home and tell my grandmother.'

The girls waited. They thought it strange that so great a chief should have to tell his grandmother, but they said nothing. The man, who was no other than Owl, ran on to his home and, calling his grandmother, said, 'Clean up the lodge and put it in order. I am going to bring home two girls whom I am playing a joke on. They think I am the rich chief and want to marry me.' After they had cleaned the lodge, for it was very disorderly, Owl said, 'I am going to put this turkey which I have brought home over my bed; when you get up in the morning ask me which turkey you shall cook and pretend to point to one, and I will say, 'No, take this.' Then the girls will think that we have many turkeys and many good things to eat.'

Owl went back for the girls and brought them to his grandmother's lodge. They were pleased, for everything looked neat and nice, and so they married Owl. Every day Owl came in with the turkey, and he always pretended to have been out hunting. Really he had been at the council, and the chief gave him the turkey for allowing him to sit on his back. At all the councils the chief always sat on Owl's back, and so he gave Owl a turkey every time to repay him for his trouble and the pain of holding him so long.

Source
George A. Dorsey, 'Traditions of the Caddo', *Carnegie Institution*, 41 (1905), pp. 67–8

After many moons the twins grew weary of nothing but turkey and they began to suspect something, so one day they followed Owl when he went away. They followed and saw him go to a large grass lodge. They peeped through an opening, and there they saw Owl sitting in the middle of the lodge with the chief sitting on his head. They gave a scream. Owl recognized their voices and jumped up, throwing the chief off his head, and ran home. He gave his grandmother a terrible scolding for letting the girls follow him and find him out. The girls felt so ashamed when they discovered how they had been fooled that they slipped off to their home and told their father and mother their experience.

TAR-BABY

Biloxi

THE RABBIT AND THE FRENCHMAN were two friends. The Rabbit aided the Frenchman, agreeing to work a piece of land on shares. The first season they planted potatoes. The Rabbit, having been told to select his share of the crop, chose the potato vines and devoured them all. The next season they planted corn. This year the Rabbit said, 'I will eat the roots.' So he pulled up all the corn by the roots, but he found nothing to satisfy his hunger. Then the Frenchman said, 'Let us dig a well.' But the Rabbit did not wish to work any longer with his friend. Said he to the Frenchman, 'If you wish to dig a well, I shall not help you.'

'Oho,' said the Frenchman, 'you shall not drink any of the water from the well.'

'That does not matter,' replied the Rabbit, 'I am accustomed to licking the dew from the ground.' The Frenchman, suspecting mischief, made a tar-baby, which he stood up close to the well. The Rabbit approached the well, carrying a long piece of cane and a tin bucket. On reaching the well he addressed the tar-baby, who remained silent.

'Friend, what is the matter? Are you angry?' said the Rabbit.

Still the tar-baby said nothing. So the Rabbit hit him with one forepaw, which stuck there.

'Let me go or I will hit you on the other side,' exclaimed the Rabbit. And when he found that the tar-baby paid no attention to him, he hit him with his other forepaw, which stuck to the tar-baby.

'I will kick you,' said the Rabbit. But when he kicked the tar-baby, the hind foot stuck.

'I will kick you with the other foot,' said the Rabbit. And when he did so, that foot, too, stuck to the tar-baby. Then the Rabbit resembled a ball, because his feet were sticking to the tar-baby and he could neither stand nor recline.

Just at this time the Frenchman approached. He tied the legs of the Rabbit together, laid him down and scolded him. Then the Rabbit pretended to be in great fear of a briar patch.

'As you are in such fear of a briar patch,' said the Frenchman, 'I will throw you into one.'

'Oh, no,' replied the Rabbit.

'I will throw you into the briar patch,' responded the Frenchman.

'I am much afraid of it,' said the Rabbit.

'As you are in such dread of it,' said the Frenchman, 'I will throw you into it.' So he seized the Rabbit and threw him into the briar patch. The Rabbit fell at some distance from the Frenchman. But instead of being injured, he sprang up and ran off, laughing at the trick which he had played on the Frenchman.

Source
J.O. Dorsey,
'Two Biloxi
Tales', *JAFL*, 6
(1893),
pp. 48–9

ALLIGATOR POWER

Choctaw

ONE WINTER THERE WERE many hunters living in a village, all of whom, with one exception, had killed a great many deer. But one had met with very poor luck and although he often succeeded in getting close to deer, just ready to draw his bow on them, they always contrived to escape unharmed. He had been away from his village three days and during that time had seen many deer, but he had not been able to kill a single one. On the third day, when the sun was overhead, the hunter saw a huge alligator resting on a dry, sandy spot.

This alligator had been without water for many days, and was dry and shrivelled and so weak that he could scarcely speak. He was able, however, to ask the hunter where water could be had. The hunter replied, 'In that forest, only a short journey hence, is a clear, deep pool of cold water.' 'But I cannot travel alone; I am too weak to go so far. Come nearer that we may talk and plan. I cannot harm you; have no fear,' said the alligator.

At last the hunter went nearer and listened to the alligator, who said, 'I know you are a hunter, but all the deer escape from you. Now, carry me to the water and I will then make you a great hunter and tell you how to kill many, many deer.' The hunter hesitated, as he feared the alligator, and then he said, 'I will carry you, but not unless I may bind your legs so you cannot scratch and your mouth so you cannot bit me.' The alligator rolled over on his back and held up his legs, saying, 'I am helpless; bind me and do with me as you will.'

The hunter lifted the bound alligator to his shoulder and carried him to the water.

Then the hunter bound with a cord the alligator's legs and mouth. Then he lifted the animal to his shoulder and carried him to the water. When they reached the pool the hunter loosened the cords and the alligator plunged into the water. It went down, then returned to the surface three times, then went down again and remained a long time. At last he rose again to the surface and spoke to the hunter, saying, 'You brought me to the water; now listen, and if you do as I counsel you will become a great hunter. Take your bow and arrows and go into the woods. You will first meet a small doe, but do not kill it. Next you will meet a large doe, but you must not shoot this one, either. Then you will see a small buck, but this likewise must be spared. Lastly you will encounter a very large, old buck. Go very close to it and kill it, and ever afterward you will be able to kill many deer.'

The hunter did as the alligator told him and never again was without venison in his camp.

Source
David Bushnell, 'The Choctaw of Bayou Lacomb, St Tammany Parish, LA', *BAEB*, 48 (1909), pp. 32–3, and John Swanton, 'Myths and Tales of the Southeastern Indians', *BAEB*, 88 (1929) p. 34

THE CELESTIAL CANOE

Alabama

MANY AGES AGO, the Alabama peoples witnessed the arrival of a magical canoe near their encampment. The canoe held several young maidens, who stepped out of the craft, joyously singing. The women ran about, freely enjoying themselves, playing a ball game with one another. When they had finished their sport, they tiredly reboarded the canoe and sailed out of sight once again. Several more times the maidens returned in their magical canoe, each time

Source
John R. Swanton, 'The Celestial Canoe', *BAE Bulletin*, 42 (1924–5), p. 138

visiting the earth near the Alabama village. Each time they sang, danced and played ball until they tired of their performance and returned into the sky aboard their sky canoe.

During one of the canoe's visits, a young Alabama warrior watched secretly as the sky maidens played and sang. While playing ball, one of the girls came close to him, fetching the ball. As she came near him, she did not know he was there. Suddenly, he jumped out from behind the bushes and grabbed her by the hand. Panic ensued among the sky visitors, and they hurried to their canoe and disappeared into the heavens, leaving one of their group behind. The Alabama warrior made the sky maiden his wife. In time, she produced several children for him. As his family grew in number, the Alabama warrior made two canoes, a large one for his family and a smaller one for just himself.

One day, his children were hungry and they spoke to their father: 'We are hungry. Will you hunt a deer and give us some fresh meat?' In response, the father headed off into the woods to hunt, but after a short span of time, he returned to his lodge with no deer in hand. At their mother's request, the children asked their father, 'Go hunt a fat deer for us.' Again, the Alabama warrior left his family to go hunt, this time intending to go further from his lodge in search of game. After he left his family and his lodge, the mother took her children and placed them in the large canoe her husband had built. She then sang her magic song and the canoe began magically to float into the sky. But the father heard the singing and returned to his lodge in time to catch the floating canoe and pull it back down to earth.

Another day, the mother repeated her attempt to escape from earth with her children. This time she placed her children in the large canoe and herself in the smaller canoe. As she sang, the canoes began to rise. Again, her husband returned from his hunting in time to take hold of the larger canoe and bring it down with his children inside. However, the mother continued her celestial song and soon floated high into the sky, until she and the canoe disappeared.

The husband soon missed his wife, as did his children. After several weeks had passed, he and his children climbed inside the large canoe and sang the song she had sung. The canoe began to float and they soon found themselves sailing through the sky and beyond the clouds. Soon, they arrived in a sky place and stepped out of their canoe. They came upon an old grandmother sitting outside her lodge. The Alabama husband asked her if she had seen his wife. 'My children wish to see their mother, for they miss her greatly.' The Old Woman spoke: 'She is over yonder, where she dances and sings continuously. If you would like to eat before you go to her, I will cook you a meal of squash.' The husband and his children decided to eat with her. Soon, she brought them a single cooked squash. As they began to eat, they knew it would not be enough for all of them. However, they were surprised when they saw that as they ate the squash, a great squash appeared in its place, as if by magic! Since they were very hungry, the man and his children ate and ate. When they finished eating, there was more food available for them. The Old Grandmother then fed the children corn.

Then the father left with his children and walked to another lodge, where he asked about his wife. 'She is here,' he was told. 'She spends all her time singing and dancing.' At that moment, the mother came dancing by her family, but she did not recognize them. Again, she danced by and this time her children tossed pieces of corn to make her notice them. Still she did not stop or notice them. The

PART 3
THE GREAT LAKES REGION

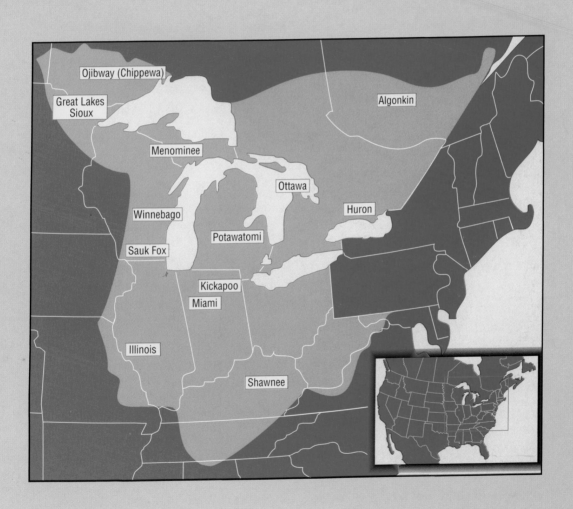

Ojibway (Chippewa)

Great Lakes Sioux

Algonkin

Menominee

Ottawa

Huron

Winnebago

Sauk Fox

Potawatomi

Kickapoo

Miami

Illinois

Shawnee

TRIBES OF THE
GREAT LAKES REGION

Anthropologists date the occupation of the Great Lakes region by human beings to approximately 10,000 BC. The ancient peoples who wandered into this region were Palaeo-Indians who hunted the great mastodons. Little evidence of these nomadic hunters exists today. What does remain are Stone Age tools and weapons. These include Clovis-style projectile points, common to many parts of North America in the Palaeolithic era. Mastodon-hunting remained the primary occupation of these hunters until about 7000 BC, when the great shaggy beasts began to die out. Changes in the climate not only brought the mastodons to the edge of extinction but changed the lifestyles of the ancient Indians.

The Great Lakes region witnessed the rise of a new anthropological age, known as the Neolithic. Between 7000 and 4500 BC the Aqua-Plano group of Native Americans dominated the region. With the disappearance of the mastodon, these Neolithic peoples continued to work with stone and hunted smaller game, including elk, caribou and deer. By 4500 BC two relatively distinct cultural groups had developed: the Boreal Archaic and the Old Copper.

The Boreal Archaic could be found from the Upper Great Lakes east to the Atlantic Ocean. This period marked the transition of Woodland Indians from an emphasis on the making of stone implements to an extended emphasis on woodworking. Thriving in the pine and hardwood forests of the Great Lakes, these Native Americans developed woodworking tools, such as axes and stone adzes. Such Neolithic axes were used for a variety of purposes, including making dug-out canoes.

Perhaps as an offshoot of the Boreal Archaic cultural group, the Copper Culture developed after 4500 BC. Reaching a peak during the millennium between 4000 and 3000 BC, it was centred

in the region of the western Great Lakes, primarily in the modern-day state of Illinois and north to Lake Superior. Here Native Americans began working raw copper into many different items. These were alternately functional, including spears, axes, knives, awls and wedges for splitting tree trunks, and decorative, resulting in the creation of copper bracelets, pendants and beads. Copper Culture Indians not only fashioned copper into tools, weapons and trinkets through hammering raw ore, they annealed the metal – a process that includes heating the ore and working the softened copper. They were also woodworkers, who built their dug-out canoes from the same lakeland forests as their Boreal neighbours.

In time, the Old Copper Culture withered away, while the Boreal Archaic group continued to develop. By 1500 BC the Boreal Archaic had given way to the Late Archaic, which marked the early stages of the Woodland Cultures. Around 3,000 years ago, the Early Woodland stage saw the advent of the Adena cultural group, which was noted for its burial mounds.

The Adena Culture spread up and down the Ohio River valley. These cultures are marked by larger population groups, an advanced style of pottery making, highly stylized cloth weaving, a more sedentary lifestyle, the development of rectangular-shaped houses and a clear delineation of status and rank among members. The Adena cultural group, however, was overshadowed by the eventual development of the Hopewellian Culture, which rose up among Woodland Indians about AD 500–700. Although the cultural age lasted only a few hundred years, these Native Americans were involved in greater trade among themselves and with their neighbours. They built elaborate burial mounds, worked implements out of stone, copper and bone, and carved intricate items of utility and pleasure, including musical instruments, tobacco pipes, eating utensils and jewellery.

Between 1000 and 1600 the Great Lakes region and the Ohio River valley tribes developed into those that were in place by the time of the arrival of the European explorers. Those tribes located in southern Wisconsin developed from the Hopewellian Culture into the Effigy Mound Culture, noted for the burial sites shaped like animals and birds. (The Great Serpent Mound in southwest Ohio is an example.) In the lands of modern-day Minnesota and the Great Lakes region, tribal groups developed, speaking a variety of languages, including dialects of Siouan, Algonquian and Iroquoian. About 1000, the Winnebago migrated from the upper Mississippi valley into northeastern Wisconsin. All such tribes were by this time practising organized agriculture, as well as relying on the hunt and fishing the myriad lakes and streams of this vast northern region. Although not all tribes fit into one generalized description or cultural group, the peoples who occupied the Great Lakes region and the lands north of the Ohio River are generally known today as those belonging to the Algonquian group.

The Algonquins

The term 'Algonquin' may be used in several different, and even confusing, ways. Linguists use the label to identify those tribes who spoke a regional variation of a major language group. From the Algonquian language stock, words familiar to English speakers today have come down to us: hickory, moccasin, moose, papoose, powwow, sachem, squash, squaw, tomahawk, totem and wigwam, for example. Others use the name to identify a large culture group located in the American Northeast, from New England west to the Great Lakes. Anthropologists divide the cultural group known as the Algonquins into subcultures, including the New England Algonquins, the Hudson River group, the Middle Atlantic group, the Southern group, the Great Lakes group, the Prairie group, the Canadian Woodland group and the Canadian Subarctic group. This chapter is concerned with the Algonquins found in the Great Lakes and Prairie

culture groups. The individual cultural groups are represented by specific tribes, each of which ranged in a limited region. Those tribes that are included in the Great Lakes group were the Chippewa, Algonquin, Menominee, Ottawa and Potawatomi. As the group name indicates, they ranged through the Lakes country, especially in the lands of modern-day Michigan. The Prairie Algonquins were the tribes Fox, Kickapoo, Sauk, Illinois, Miami and Shawnee, whose homes were usually to be found in modern-day Wisconsin, Illinois and Indiana. These and other Algonquins were among the first Indians to make contact with the British and French explorers and settlers of the seventeenth and eighteenth centuries. Traditionally, the Algonquins became allies of the French in Canada, while their neighbours in the Northeast, the Iroquois, allied themselves with the British. Throughout the seventeenth and eighteenth centuries the slow but continuous movement of whites pushed the Algonquins further west. The Great Lakes Algonquins were among the last of the subcultural groups to feel this pressure, but they too, by the nineteenth century, found themselves being removed by the United States government to relocation sites, primarily reservations in Oklahoma.

Algonquian Society

In looking at the Algonquian lifestyle and social structure, it is possible to see a reliance on intertribal confederacies. These unions often provided the military structure for protecting the tribes, as well as the legal system for their members. Such confederacies were not as well organized as neighbouring Iroquois unions, serving rather as a loose connection between Algonquian villages and towns.

Most such confederacies were led by a grand sachem, a chief of great wisdom and varying authority. Grand sachems in some villages had power no greater than that of a mediator of disputes, while in others they might have the power of an almighty monarch. However, most Algonquian tribes in the Great Lakes region were led, instead, by a dual leadership of two chiefs, one a war chief and the other a peace chief. War chiefs were chosen by the tribe's membership, while the position of peace chief was often hereditary.

Some Great Lakes Algonquian tribes had a third chief who was a shaman, a holy medicine man who organized and led the tribe's religious ceremonies.

Tribal organization among the Algonquins often included bands comprising extended families who hunted and lived together throughout the year. A tribe's bands traditionally came together each summer for important celebrations and ceremonies. Even when the band structure was in place among a tribe's members, an essential element of tribal social organization was the moiety. Moieties resulted in the dividing of clans into two groups; each was responsible for various functions within a tribe. They also served as the opposing teams during a tribe's sporting games. Families who intermarried within a tribe were generally part of the same clan, another subdivision of a band. Such clans often identified themselves through symbols such as animals or elements. These symbols were known as totems. Totems were considered sacred by their clan and thought to have great power, as well as providing protection for band members.

Algonquian Wigwams

As has already been discussed earlier in this book (see page 14), typical housing among Algonquian tribes was the rounded, bark-covered wigwam. We shall take time now to elaborate on the subject here.

Generally, there were three different types of wigwam: domed, conical and an extended conical pattern. The domed wigwam was found among the Chippewas. The structure was circular or oval and measured about fifteen feet (five metres) in diameter. Approximately eighteen to twenty saplings were used to build the wigwam's framework, with the poles set approximately two feet (just under a metre) apart. The poles were bent into the circle's centre and those opposite each other were lashed together with strips of cedar bark, forming supporting arches.

Wigwams were covered with a natural sheathing. Often, cat's tails were sewn together to form the walls of the wigwam, while strips of bark were placed on top of the lashed poles to form a roof for the dwelling. Various woods were used, but birch was considered ideal. This wood

was light and hearty, and the birch pieces were easily removed, rolled up and transported when a band uprooted and moved to a new campsite. Such a dwelling was relatively cool in summer. When winter came, the Algonquins covered the wigwams with an additional layer of bark over the outer walls, piled mountains of autumn leaves all around their houses and stacked evergreen branches on top and around the entire structure.

At the top of these primitive yet snug houses, a smoke hole was left open so that the home's campfire might emit its smoke. Inside the wigwam, woven mats of cat's tails covered the floor. Additional mats provided bedding.

The second variety of wigwam, called the conical wigwam, was not used by the Algonquins of the Great Lakes region but by tribes located in New England. This wigwam resembled the tepees of the Great Plains tribes, but was covered with sections of birch bark rather than buffalo hides.

The third type, called by the Chippewa *wigwassawigamig*, was found commonly among the Algonquins. Anthropologists refer to this as an 'extended conical' because of its shape. Rather than the framework consisting of poles stacked together in the shape of a cone, a *wigwassawigamig* featured a ridge pole about six to eight feet (two to three metres) in length, with poles leaning into it, providing the frame for the wigwam. This house, like the other two types of wigwams, was also covered in sheets of birch bark.

The Algonquins built other lodges, some smaller and some quite large. Each had a specific purpose. Smaller wigwams might serve as sweat lodges or places where shamans prophesied. Larger lodges provided the meeting houses for the bands. Often these larger structures stood twenty to thirty feet (seven to nine metres) in width and were 200 feet (sixty metres) in length. Such buildings served to house all the members of a large band of Algonquins.

When the Algonquins built their villages, they provided protection for their homes and families by erecting a palisade or stockade around their encampment. Such 'forts' were either circular or square and often featured drainage ditches around them to keep rainwater from flooding a village site.

Food Sources

The Algonquian tribes practised a combination of hunting, formal agriculture, gathering and fishing to feed themselves. They did not raise any domesticated animals for eating, although they used dogs on hunting expeditions. Hunters and fishermen provided fresh meat, especially in non-winter months. Large and small animals alike filled the cooking pots and fire pots of the Algonquins. Deer was a mainstay, as well as bear, moose and elk. Tribes to the north hunted caribou too. Smaller animals, such as rabbit, squirrel and even beaver, were hunted, and gamebirds – duck, goose, turkey and partridge – were hunted and trapped.

Traps included snares and deadfalls, these latter used in killing larger animals. A typical deadfall involved the erection of a pair of logs standing on end with a third post – sometimes called a samson post by Europeans – resting on the ends of the support posts. The end of a large log was placed gingerly across the support pole. The entire contraption was designed to collapse at the slightest touch. Bait was placed beneath the large log. Many an unwary bear or deer set off such traps. Snares were used typically to catch small animals and gamebirds. A limber tree sapling was bent over and attached to a trigger device, then a piece of cord or rope was set in a loop on the ground below the trigger. Bait was set on the opposite end of the trigger and when a gamebird, for example, wandered by and took the bait, the trigger was sprung, the sapling jerked up and, it was hoped, snagged the bird.

While hunters on land chased down or captured their quarry, Algonquian fishermen traversed the lakes, rivers and streams of the region to catch fish. The Great Lakes teemed with fish; the sturgeon was the largest, weighing hundreds of pounds. These fishermen used a variety of methods in their work, including nets, traps, spears and harpoons. They ran lines with hooks on their ends, fashioned from bone or antler. Bird wishbones were used to make crude fish hooks. The Algonquins also caught larger fish using bone gorges – straight pieces of bone with their ends sharpened and the fishing line tied in the bone's centre. When the fish took in the gorge, it turned sideways after being swallowed,

leaving them caught on the line. The Algonquins trapped eels for food as well. This activity usually took place in the spring, when the eels migrated. To catch them, the Indians built weirs, or wooden fences, across shallow streams, so that their prey was funnelled into narrow chutes flanked by waiting fishermen in dug-out canoes. The shallow, narrow waters were difficult for the eels to manoeuvre in and they were caught in large numbers. Once the eels were speared, the women on shore skinned them and smoked them over low fires.

Among the domesticated crops raised by the Algonquins were corn, beans and squash, the most common crops of the Native Americans, as well as pumpkins. A band's summer encampment was generally located on a site where at least limited farming could be carried out. Corn, beans and squash were often planted side by side, with bean vines clinging to corn stalks, snaking their way ever upwards.

Because corn was grown among the Algonquian groups, hominy was a natural food they produced. Hominy is made by cooking whole ears of corn with wood ash or lye. Once cooked, the corn hulls were picked off and washed to remove the lye, before the removed hulls were boiled again.

They also collected wild berries, such as cranberries and blueberries, roots and other edible plants. Where freshwater lakes and ponds were located, the Algonquins harvested wild rice. This 'wild' plant was eaten extensively by the tribes of the Great Lakes region. They gathered the stalks of rice, beating them with wooden sticks. This caused the grain to fall to the bottom of their canoes, which were lined with reed mats for collecting the rice. Since the Algonquins competed with the water gamebirds for rice, they harvested it just before it was fully ripe. It was then dried and threshed by being stamped on. The women of the tribes stored the grain in birch-bark storage containers, which were buried underground, where the grain might be kept many months before being eaten.

Algonquins sweetened their meals by tapping maple trees for their sap, from which they produced both maple syrup and sugar. The work was done by the women and children of each band. A maple tree was gashed along one side and flat spiles were driven into the cut. These spiles, or spouts, became the conduits for the tree's sap, which oozed into birch-bark containers. The women then boiled the sap until it produced syrup or continued the heating process until it crystallized, creating maple sugar. Many Algonquins used water to dilute maple syrup, producing a sweet drink. Sometimes the liquid was fermented, making an alcohol, but this custom was not common.

Cooking these various food stuffs and meats was generally kept simple. Freshly slain meat was skewered on green sticks and grilled over an open fire. Meat was occasionally fried, but this technique was not popular among most bands and may have been learned from their European neighbours. Algonquin women hung cooking skins over their fires, boiling the meat inside. Wooden cooking vessels were also suspended over a cooking fire on a stick, the opposite end of which was anchored by a heavy stone.

Transportation

Before the arrival of the Europeans in the New World, Native Americans did not use horses for transportation. The tribes of the Great Lakes region did have a natural advantage in developing a viable transport system thanks to the many lakes and rivers that cut through their homelands. They were able to make use of these by building canoes, which were small, lightweight, sleek and reasonably manoeuvrable.

Just as the Great Plains tribes were noted for their tepees, eagle-feather bonnets and horse-bound buffalo hunts, the Northeastern tribes, including the Algonquins, were noted for their birch-bark canoes. By paddling their canoes, the Lakes country Native Americans could travel great distances, going far from home.

Canoes did not come in a standard size or design. Some were built with low bows and sterns, and these were ideal for travel on calmer rivers since they were sleek and fast, their design exerting little wind resistance. Others were built for plying the waters of the Great Lakes and other large bodies of water, where the waves might be sharper and higher. There, the canoes were built with high bows and sterns. The length of a canoe also varied widely. A common model

was built to accommodate two people at best, while longer designs resulted in a canoe that could hold as many as ten, sitting in rows of two abreast. Northeastern and Great Lakes canoes varied, then, from ten or twelve feet (three or four metres) in length to fifty or sixty feet (fifteen to eighteen metres).

Native American canoes were built from several different types of wood – spruce, elm and especially birch. Bark was peeled directly from standing trees in lengthy strips and sections. A typical canoe's framework was made from pieces of white cedar, since this wood splits easily. The frame was then covered with birch-bark pieces. Birch bark did not change its shape through stretching or shrinking. The pieces were laced together with strips of split roots of black spruce. Black-spruce gum was then heated until it had the consistency of a thickish syrup before being spread over the canoe's seams and cracks, to make them watertight. The insides of these canoes were lined with strips of white cedar. Bow-shaped sticks of cedar or maple were placed across the canoe's middle length to give the canoe a wider shape across its gunwales. Paddles were often carved out of maple as well.

Building even such a simple craft was not a one-day task. Canoe-building generally required the efforts of at least two men and perhaps four women, working for two to three weeks. The women harvested and prepared the spruce for the boat and were responsible for sewing and sealing the birch-bark pieces. Once completed, these crafts were light enough for a man to carry one measuring as long as eighteen feet. Inside a typical canoe, Indians kept a birch-bark 'bucket' for bailing out water, spare pieces of birch bark and spruce root and pine gum for emergency repairs, and a heavy stone tied to a piece of cordage for use as an anchor. When paddling a canoe, Algonquins sat in the bottom of the boat, often on a deer skin. Rarely did these crafts have any seats.

Algonquian Clothing

As with all other Native American tribes, the Algonquins wore as many clothes as they needed to suit the weather. In the warm and humid summer months, most Indians wore less than in the colder seasons. Children generally wore no clothing until they reached the age of ten. By then they were considered adults.

The women of the Ohio country and Great Lakes tribes generally wore dresses of deer skin, hemmed below the knee. Such dresses were wrapped around a woman and held in place by a belt. Women wore leather leggings in the winter and typically wore moccasins all year round. Also, in cool weather the women wore pairs of cape sleeves, which were joined at the back of the neck. Often such clothing – dresses, skirts, capes – was fringed.

Most Algonquian men wore less than the women, regardless of the weather. A typical summertime costume was a breechclout and moccasins, although footwear was optional. Such breechclouts were mere strips of leather, approximately three feet (one metre) in width, which were run through a leather belt and between the warrior's thighs. However, if a day's activities were to be spent in the forests, a brave often wore leggings for protection. Leggings were not necessarily the same as trousers, however. Some leggings came up to only just below the knees; others covered the thighs as well.

In winter Algonquian men wore fur skins for warmth. Robes of fur were draped over the shoulders and might be supplemented on extremely cold days with rabbit-skin blankets. To help them walk through snowy landscapes, Algonquian men wore moose-hide boots, sometimes over their moccasins. Such boots were cut and sewn from the hind leg of a moose, just where the animal's hock bends. This provided the boots with a natural heel. Moccasins might also be stuffed with padding to help keep a brave's feet warm, with deer or moose hair or cat's-tail fluff being used most often.

Moccasins were worn all year round and were typically of two different designs. One was constructed from a single piece of leather, cut and sewn down the middle to make footwear that was slightly boot-shaped. The other model, which mirrored the more modern concept of the moccasin, was sewn from three pieces of deer-skin. It included stitching that formed the puckered moccasin top, plus a thin band of hide sewn in a tube along the moccasin's heel. A leather drawstring was run through the tube which could be tightened and tied to make the footwear fit more snugly.

In addition to wearing moccasins, Algonquins wore snow-shoes in winter. These lightweight 'shoes' were attached to the moccasins or fur boots and were sometimes up to three feet (one metre) in length. Snow-shoes were cut from a green piece of wood, generally ash, which formed the frame. This wooden strip was heated and bent in the shape of either a large teardrop or an oval. An intricate pattern of thwarts and meshing filled in the space of the shoe. Commonly, men's snow-shoes featured two thwarts, one that crossed in front of the wearer's toes and the other behind the heel of his moccasin. Sinew was then woven beneath the moccasin to provide support. Additional webbing was included both behind and in front of the moccasin, with the closest netting in front to keep the snow off the wearer's foot as much as possible. A leather thong curved above the middle of the snow-shoe to hold the moccasin in place while walking.

Women and children wore a different model of snow-shoe called a 'bear-paw'. These shoes were smaller and designed for short walks within the camp. They were barely eighteen inches (fifty centimetres) long, about one foot (thirty centimetres) in width and were oval-shaped, with the shoe's front slightly wider than the back. These shoes were less elaborate and did not have nearly as much webbing as did the warrior's snow-shoe.

Men and women alike decorated their clothing with paints, feathers, freshwater shells and porcupine quills. Often, they dyed their feathers in vegetable and wood-root shades to give them a more colourful appearance. They sometimes created elaborate patterns with paints and quills. Contact with whites later allowed them to replace quills and shells with glass beads.

Algonquian Headgear and Hairstyles

Algonquian men and women did not tend towards elaborate head-dresses or feathered bonnets, as was the custom of other Native American tribes, although how they displayed their hair was of great importance to them. Hair for the

Algonquins was a symbol of independence and individual power.

Hairstyles varied between men and women. The women generally wore their hair in braids, topped with a smallish cap or headband of decorated shells. The men wore a variety of styles, depending on the custom of their individual tribes, bands and clans. Some men wore their hair long, tied off in two braids or pulled up into two great hanks of hair, minus the braids. Others affected the roach cut, which required braves to pluck out their hair except for a wide strip left running down the middle of the scalp from the forehead to the nape of the neck

Often Algonquin men maintained a scalp lock, a longer piece of hair left in the middle of the roach. This extra length of hair was maintained for the convenience of, and perhaps as a taunt for, any enemy who might have opportunity to scalp a brave in battle. Scalp locks were treated in various fashions, from simply letting them fall loose, dangling down from the roach, to tying them up so that they stood above the general hair line of the roach.

In winter, both men and women wore a variety of fur caps. Occasionally they wore an entire fur skin, complete with the head of the animal, such as a fox or otter. These caps were tied around the sides of the head, leaving the top of the head exposed. This type of headgear may have been the progenitor of the racoon cap that was worn by American pioneers and frontiersmen of the eighteenth and early nineteenth centuries.

As for feathers as hair decorations, the Algonquins did not wear them often or in any considerable numbers. Warriors recognized for their valour in combat might wear a single feather on their heads. Such a feather might be cut in such a way so as to indicate a specific deed in battle. Unlike the Indians of the Great Plains, the Algonquins did not accumulate feathers as symbolic trophies or make elaborate eagle-feather bonnets.

Algonquins at War

When the Algonquins went to war, they approached the art in much the same way as their neighbours. Generalized war between the tribe and a neighbour, whether another tribe or a white settlement, was organized by tribal leaders or by the leaders of established raiding parties. Such fighting did not usually include large warring parties or what might be called large-scale battles. Raiding was a common activity, and one that consumed much of a brave's time and effort. Generally, raids against a neighbouring tribe were organized by one warrior, often called a war leader, and planned against a specific enemy band or group. Such raids were carried out for singular purposes as well, including gaining new hunting lands at the expense of an enemy, acquiring honour among fellow tribesmen or as an act of vengeance for the death of another brave.

War leaders could come from any rank of a tribe's warriors. Such a brave outlined his strategy with fellow tribesmen and assumed responsibility for the raid's success. Before others agreed to follow him, they first had to feel that he was the possessor of Manitou. It was supernatural in nature but was considered to be a spiritual quality rather than a spirit itself. Both spiritual beings and humans could possess it, in much the same way that modern culture speaks of the human spirit. A war leader gained access to Manitou through a vision, and its possession was considered good for one military raid only. Any warrior who went on a raid did so by his own choice; no one could be forced to participate. Any volunteer warrior could abandon the expedition at any time of his choosing short of the actual raid itself.

Raids were often conducted far from the encampment, so the raiding party would spend several days in the forests making their way to the designated target. The advance was often slow, with warriors killing game along the way and storing the meat to consume on the way back. If a raiding party consisted of a couple of dozen braves, a sacred bundle was often taken to provide a measure of spiritual protection. With smaller parties, the war leader's personal bundle was considered adequate.

Once a raiding party located its enemy, the warriors usually made their assault as a surprise attack. If the raid was a success, the warrior who made the first kill led the group back. If the party had been defeated, the return was often disorganized, with every man for himself. During a raid, captives might be taken and brought back to the party's camp to serve as slaves. If a captive was old, he was usually killed on the trip back. When a successful war party returned to its people, a scalp dance was held, with a great feast for the returning warriors.

Algonquian Weaponry

As with many tribes in North America before the arrival of the Europeans, the chief weapon used by the Algonquins was the bow and arrow. A typical Algonquian bow was a straight, flat piece of wood measuring about five feet (1.5 metres) in length. The bow was about two inches (five centimetres) wide and half an inch (one centimetre) thick. The bow tapered on both ends where notches held the bowstring. Bows were often made from ash, hickory, red cedar and white oak. Bowstrings were made from deer sinew and other natural plant fibres. Some were even made from the neck skin of snapping turtles, a material prized in the making of bowstrings since it neither shrank nor stretched out of shape.

A warrior considered his bow to be an extension of himself and protected his weapon with extreme care. When carving a bow, a warrior first cut a piece of bow wood from a tree and then began working it, giving it its rudimentary shape. Then he rubbed bear grease on the unfinished piece and hung it inside his lodge, letting the wood season for several months. During those months, the warrior would periodically regrease it. When a bow was completed, it was handled with great respect. When not in use, bows were unstrung and kept in protective cases. Warriors continued to lubricate their bows with oil even when not in use. Long before they were of an age to be warriors, Algonquian boys carved small bows, learning, then perfecting their craft over their entire lifetimes. Warriors considered too old for the hunt or for warring raids often continued their work in making bows and also arrows.

Arrows were cut from several kinds of tree noted for their straight branches, including dogwood trees and the viburnum bush, which often went by the name of arrow-wood. Even branches that were not naturally straight were heated and bent into shape using a special tool designed for just such a purpose. Arrowheads were usually knapped from stone, but other materials were also used, including animal bone, slate, shell fragments and copper. Such arrowheads were carved to the appropriate shape and usually lashed on to the wooden shaft with sinew. Arrows were sometimes carved so that a bulbous portion of wood, called a bunt, was left on the end of the shaft, giving the arrow a natural head. These arrows were used to hunt birds and small game, and would stun the animal rather than cut through its body.

To give the arrow its trueness in flight, warriors cut strips of feathers and attached them to the opposite end of the wooden shaft. Most arrows featured three split feathers spaced evenly around the shaft's tail end. These were glued in place with spruce gum, the same material used to waterproof canoes. Arrows were kept in buckskin quivers hung behind a warrior's left shoulder blade. Accompanying the quiver was the warrior's bow case, which was generally decorated and fringed.

Algonquian Religion

The world of spirits and the supernatural was of great significance to the Algonquian tribes. As has already been stated, the concept central to the spirit life of Algonquins was that of Manitou. This was considered highly sacred, an abstract force that in some mysterious fashion determined whether a person's efforts were to be successful or not. Warriors tapped into the spirit world of Manitou by fasting, sometimes for several days, looking for some sign of the presence of the force, perhaps a visitation or vision from the spirit world. Even when one had the blessing of the Manitou, it was not permanent; one had to receive it over and over to continue to have spiritual confidence and to complete noteworthy tasks.

The Algonquins made medicine bundles for themselves, as was the custom with other regional culture groups. In such bundles the warrior kept items he had seen in his visions as symbols that helped him to make connection with the spirit world.

Kitshi Manitou and Wisagatcak

While Manitou was considered a spiritual quality that humans could achieve, the Algonquins recognized a great and powerful spirit that they called Kitshi, or Gitche Manitou. This being was the supreme god of the Algonquins. In addition, they recognized another god, named Wisagatcak, who was the creator of the world.

Stories abound about the trickster Wisagatcak, who built a pole fence across a river where he intended to trap the giant beaver. At the end of the day, Wisagatcak saw him swimming close by. As he prepared to spear the beaver, the muskrat bit Wisagatcak, causing his throw to go wild. Discouraged, Wisagatcak decided to give up on killing the giant beaver, so he began to tear down his wooden dam. As the dam came down, the river's waters poured out but the water level of the river did not recede. The giant beavers were causing the water to flow endlessly in torrents, flooding all the surrounding land.

To save himself and the nearby animals, Wisagatcak uprooted some trees and constructed himself a raft. He then collected many animals, rescuing them from the swirling waters. The giant beavers continued to make the waters flow, and Wisagatcak floated on his raft with his animals for two weeks. The muskrat then left the raft and dived under the water to see if he could find land. He couldn't and subsequently drowned. The raven was released from the raft to look for dry land, but could not find any. Wisagatcak then enlisted the help of the wolf, who began running around the raft with a wad of moss in his mouth. While he ran, the moss began to grow, with clumps of earth attached. Wisagatcak then cast a powerful spell on the moss and it spread out until it became a new world. This story was common among the Cree Indians of the north.

Another spirit important in the Algonquin was the heroic figure Glooscap, who has already been mentioned (see page 16). Creation stories also credit him with making the world.

Nature and the Spiritual World

For the Algonquins, the natural and the spiritual or supernatural world were always inextricably linked. The sun and moon were Manitous, specifically the grandfather and grandmother of some tribes. The stars of the Milky Way formed a river in the sky, while other stars represented the dead and departed spirits of Algonquian ancestors. To the Algonquins, the four stars of the Big Dipper symbolized a bear, while the other three stars of the Dipper's handle represented three hunters chasing the bear through the otherwise black heavens. Each autumn the hunter spirits killed the bear. When his blood dripped down to earth, it turned the leaves of the trees red. This idea was part of a never-ending cycle of life and death in the spiritual world of the Algonquins.

Algonquian Witchcraft

Like many other North American tribes, the Algonquins believed in the presence of supernatural beings called witches. Witches were imagined as both male and female. Such spirits travelled about at night, making a hissing noise as they went along. Fire flashed from their mouths, lighting up the night sky. Witches performed acts of evil on both nature and humans, often receiving the blame for any tragedy that befell an individual or his or her tribe which could not be explained otherwise. So, for example, unexplained deaths were blamed on witches, as were diseases and body swellings.

MYTHS AND LEGENDS
OF THE GREAT LAKES REGION

THE STAR-MAIDEN

Chippewa

A YOUNG WARRIOR NAMED ALGON was walking over the prairies. On his way, he discovered a circular pathway, worn as if by the tread of many feet, though there were no footmarks visible outside its bounds. The young hunter, who had never before encountered one of these 'fairy rings', was filled with surprise at the discovery, and hid himself in the long grass to see whether an explanation might not be forthcoming. He had not long to wait. In a little while he heard the sound of music, so faint and sweet that it surpassed anything he had ever dreamed of. The strains grew fuller and richer, and as they seemed to come from above he turned his eyes towards the sky. Far in the blue he could see a tiny white speck like a floating cloud. Nearer and nearer it came, and the astonished hunter saw that it was no cloud, but a dainty willow basket, in which were seated twelve beautiful maidens. The music he had heard was the sound of their voices as they sang strange and magical songs. Descending into the charmed ring, they danced round and round with such exquisite grace and abandon that it was a sheer delight to watch them. But after the first moments of dazzled surprise Algon had eyes only for the youngest of the group, a slight, vivacious creature, so fragile and delicate that it seemed to the stalwart hunter that a breath would blow her away.

He was, indeed, seized with a fierce passion for the dainty sprite, and he speedily decided to spring from the grass and carry her off. But the pretty creatures were too quick for him. The fairy of his choice skilfully eluded his grasp and rushed to the basket. The others followed, and in a moment they were soaring up in the air, singing a sweet, unearthly song. The disconsolate hunter returned to his lodge, but try as he might he could not get the thought of the Star-maiden out of his head, and next day, long before the hour of the fairies' arrival, he lay in the grass awaiting the sweet sounds that would herald their approach. At length the willow basket appeared. The twelve ethereal beings danced as before. Again Algon made a desperate attempt to seize the youngest, and again he was unsuccessful.

'Let us stay,' said one of the Star-maidens. 'Perhaps the mortal wishes to teach us his earthly dances.' But the youngest sister would not hear of it, and they all rose out of sight in their willow basket.

Poor Algon returned home more unhappy than ever. All night he lay awake dreaming of the pretty, elusive creature who had wound a chain of gossamer round his heart and brain, and early in the morning he repaired to the enchanted spot. Casting about for some means of gaining his end, he came upon the hollow trunk of a tree in which a number of mice played. With the aid of the charms in his sacred

Source

Lewis Spence,
*North American
Indians*, London:
George G.
Harrap & Co.,
1914,
pp. 152–6

bundle, he turned himself into one of these little animals, thinking the fair sisters would never pierce his disguise.

That day when the willow basket descended its occupants alighted and danced merrily as they were wont in the magic circle, till the youngest saw the hollow tree-trunk (which had not been there on the previous day) and turned to fly. Her sisters laughed at her fears, and tried to reassure her by overturning the tree trunk. The mice scampered in all directions, and were quickly pursued by the Star-maidens, who killed them all except Algon. The latter regained his own shape just as the youngest fairy raised her hand to strike him. Clasping her in his arms, he bore her to his village, while her frightened sisters ascended to their Star-country.

Arrived at his home, Algon married the maiden, and by his kindness and gentleness soon won her affection. However, her thoughts still dwelt on her own people, and though she indulged her sorrow only in secret, lest it should trouble her husband, she never ceased to lament her lost home.

One day while she was out with her little son she made a basket of willows, like the one in which she had first come to earth. Gathering together some flowers and gifts for the Star-people, she took the child with her into the basket, sang the magical songs she still remembered, and soon floated up to her own country, where she was welcomed by the king, her father.

Algon's grief was bitter indeed when he found that his wife and child had left him. But he had no means of following them. Every day he would go to the magic circle on the prairie and give vent to his sorrow, but the years went past and there was no sign of his dear ones returning.

Meanwhile the woman and her son had almost forgotten Algon and the Earth-country. However, when the boy grew old enough to hear the story he wished to go and see his father. His mother consented, and arranged to go with him. While they were preparing to descend, the Star-people said, 'Bring Algon with you when you return, and ask him to bring some feature from every beast and bird he has killed in the hunt.'

Algon, who had lately spent almost all his time at the charmed circle, was overjoyed to see his wife and son come back to him, and willingly agreed to go with them to the Star-country. He worked very hard to obtain a specimen of all the rare and curious birds and beasts in his land, and when at last he had gathered the relics – a claw of one, a feather of another, and so on – he piled them in the willow basket, climbed in himself with his wife and boy, and set off to the Star-country.

The people there were delighted with the curious gifts Algon had brought them, and, being permitted by their king to take one apiece, they did so. Those who took a tail or a claw of any beast at once became the quadruped represented by the fragment, and those who took the wings of birds became birds themselves. Algon and his wife and son took the feathers of a white falcon and flew down to the prairies, where their descendants may still be seen.

Descending into the charmed ring the fairies danced round and round with exquisite grace and abandon.

IOSCO, OR THE PRAIRIE BOY'S VISIT TO THE SUN AND MOON

Ottawa

ONE PLEASANT MORNING, five young men and a boy about ten years of age called Isoco went out a-shooting with their bows and arrows. They left their lodges with the first appearance of daylight and, having passed through a long reach of woods, had ascended a high hill before the sun arose. While standing there in a group, the sun suddenly burst forth in all its glory. The air was so clear that it appeared to be at no great distance.

'How very near it is,' they all said.

'It cannot be far,' said the eldest, 'and if you will accompany me, we will see if we cannot reach it.'

A loud assent burst from every lip. Even the boy, Iosco, said he would go. They told him he was too young, but he replied, 'If you do not permit me to go with you, I will tell your plan to each of your parents.' They then said to him, 'You shall also go with us, so be quiet.'

They then fell upon the following arrangement. It was resolved that each one should obtain from his parents as many pairs of moccasins as he could, and also new clothing of leather. They fixed on a spot where they would conceal all their articles, until they were ready to start on their journey, and which would serve, in the meantime, as a place of rendezvous, where they might secretly meet and consult. This being arranged, they returned home.

A long time passed before they could put their plan into execution. But they kept it a profound secret, even to the boy. They frequently met at the appointed place and discussed the subject. At length everything was in readiness and they decided on a day to set out. That morning the boy shed tears for a pair of new leather leggings.

'Don't you see,' said he to his parents, 'how my companions are dressed?' This appealed to their pride and envy prevailed. He obtained the leggings.

Artifices were also resorted to by the others, under the plea of going out on a special hunt. They said to one another, but in a tone that they might be overheard, 'We will see who will bring in the most game.' They went out in different directions, but soon met at the appointed place, where they had hidden the articles for their journey, with as many arrows as they had time to make. Each one took something on his back and they began their march.

They travelled day after day, through a thick forest, but the sun was always at the same distance.

'We must,' said they, 'travel towards Waubunong, the east, and we shall get to the object, some time or other.' No one was discouraged, although winter overtook them. They built a lodge and hunted till they obtained as much dried meat as they could carry and then continued on. This they did several times; season followed season. More than one winter overtook them. Yet none of them became discouraged or expressed dissatisfaction.

One day the travellers came to the banks of a river whose waters ran towards the east. They followed it down many days. As they were walking one day, they came to rising ground, from which they saw something white or clear through the trees. They encamped on this elevation. Next morning they came, suddenly, in

Source

Henry R. Schoolcraft, *North American Indian Legends*, Philadelphia: J.B. Lippincott & Co., 1856, pp. 278–91 view of an immense body of water. No land could be seen as far as the eye could reach. One or two of them lay down on the beach to drink. As soon as they got the water in their mouths, they spat it out and exclaimed, with surprise, 'Shewetagon awbo! – salt water'. It was the sea.

While looking on the water, the sun arose as if from the deep, and went on its steady course through the heavens, enlivening the scene with its cheering and animating beams. They stood in admiration, but the object appeared to be as distant from them as ever. They thought it best to encamp and consult whether it were advisable to go on or return.

'We see,' said the leader, 'that the sun is still on the opposite side of this great water, but let us not be disheartened. We can walk around the shore.' To this they all assented.

Next morning they took the northerly shore, to walk around it, but had gone only a short distance when they came to a large river. They again encamped and, while sitting before the fire, the question was put, whether any one of them had ever dreamed of water, or of walking on it. After a long silence, the eldest said he had. Soon after, they lay down to sleep.

When they arose the following morning, the eldest addressed them: 'We have done wrong in coming north. Last night my spirit appeared to me and told me to go south, and that but a short distance beyond the spot we left yesterday, we should come to a river with high banks. That by looking off its mouth, we should see an island which would approach to us. He directed that we should all get on it. He then told me to cast my eyes towards the water. I did so, and I saw all he had declared. He then informed me that we must return south and wait at the river until the day after tomorrow. I believe all that was revealed to me in this dream and that we shall do well to follow it.'

The party immediately retraced their footsteps in exact obedience to this dream. Towards the evening they came to the borders of the indicated river. It had high banks, behind which they encamped, and here they patiently awaited the fulfilment of the dream. The appointed day arrived. They said, 'We will see if that which has been said will be seen. Midday is the promised time.' Early in the morning two had gone to the shore to keep a look-out. They waited anxiously for the middle of the day, straining their eyes to see if they could discover anything. Suddenly they raised a shout, 'Ewaddee suh neen!' – There it is! There it is!'

On rushing to the spot, they beheld something like an island steadily advancing towards the shore. As it approached, they could discover that something was moving on it in various directions. They said, 'It is a Manito, let us be off into the woods.'

'No, no,' cried the eldest, 'let us stay and watch.'

It now became stationary and lost much of its imagined height. They could see only three trees, as they thought, resembling trees in a pinery that had been burned. The wind, which had been off the sea, now died away into a perfect calm. They saw something leaving the fancied island and approaching the shore, throwing and flapping its wings, like a loon when he attempts to fly in calm weather. It entered the mouth of the river.

They were on the point of running away, but the eldest dissuaded them. 'Let us hide in this hollow,' he said, 'and we will see what it can be.' They did so. They soon heard the sounds of chopping, and quickly after they heard the falling of trees. Suddenly a man came up to the place of their concealment. He stood still and gazed at them. They did the same in utter amazement. After looking at them for some time, the person advanced and extended his hand towards them. The eldest took it and they shook hands. He then spoke, but they could not understand each other. He then cried out for his comrades. They came and examined very minutely the dress of the travellers.

They again tried to converse. Finding it impossible, the strangers then motioned to the *naubequon*, a small boat, wishing them to embark. They consulted with each other for a short time. The eldest then motioned that they should go on board. They embarked on board the boat, which they found to be loaded with wood. When they reached the side of the supposed island, they were surprised to see a great number of people, who all came to the side and looked at them with open mouths. One spoke out, above the others, and appeared to be the leader. He motioned them to get on board. He looked at and examined them, and took them down into the cabin and set things before them to eat. He treated them very kindly.

When they came on deck again, all the sails were spread and they were fast losing sight of land. In the course of the night and the following day, they were sick at the stomach, but soon recovered. When they had been out at sea ten days, they became sorrowful, as they could not converse with the strangers – those who had hats on.

The following night Iosco dreamed that his spirit appeared to him. He told him not to be discouraged, that he would open his ears, so as to be able to understand the people with hats. 'I will not permit you to understand much,' said he, 'only sufficient to reveal your wants, and to know what is said to you.' Isoco repeated this dream to his friends, and they were satisfied and encouraged by it. When they had been out about thirty days, the master of the ship motioned them to change their dresses of leather for such as his people wore; for if they did not, his master would be displeased. It was on this occasion that the elder first understood a few words of the language. The first phrase he understood was *La Que notte*, and from one word to another he was soon able to speak it.

One day the men cried out, 'Land!' and soon after they heard a noise resembling thunder, in repeated peals. When they had got over their fears, they were shown the large guns which made this noise. Soon after, they saw a vessel smaller than their own, sailing out of a bay, in the direction towards them. She had flags on her masts, and when she came near she fired a gun. The large vessel also hoisted her flags, and the boat came alongside. The master told the person who came in it to tell his master or king that he had six travellers on board, such as had never been seen before, and that they were coming to visit him. It was some time after the departure of this messenger before the vessel got up to the town. It was then dark, but they could see people, and horses, and vehicles ashore. They were landed and placed in a covered vehicle, and driven off. When they stopped, they were taken into a large and splendid room. They were here told that the great chief wished to see them. They were shown into another large room, filled with men and women. All the room was of massive silver.

The chief asked them their business and the object of their journey. They told him where they were from, and where they were going, and the nature of the enterprise which they had undertaken. He tried to dissuade them from its execution, telling them of the many trials and difficulties they would have to undergo; that so many days' march from his country dwelt a bad spirit, or Manito, who foreknew and foretold the existence and arrival of all who entered his country. It is impossible, he said, my children, for you ever to arrive at the object you are in search of.

Iosco replied, 'Nosa,' and they could see the chief blush in being called father, 'we have come so far on our way, and we will continue it; we have resolved firmly that we will do so. We think our lives are of no value, for we have given them up for this object. 'Nosa,' he repeated, 'do not then prevent us from going on our journey.' The chief then dismissed them with valuable presents, after having appointed the next day to speak to them again, and provided everything that they needed or wished for.

Next day they were again summoned to appear before the king. He again tried to dissuade them. He said he would send them back to their country in one of his vessels; but all he said had no effect.

'Well,' said he, 'if you will go, I will furnish you all that is needed for your journey.' He had everything provided accordingly. He told them that three days before they reached the bad spirit he had warned them of, they would hear his rattle. He cautioned them to be wise, for he felt that he should never see them all again.

They resumed their journey and travelled sometimes through villages, but they soon left them behind and passed over a region of forests and plains, without inhabitants. They found that all the productions of the new country, trees, animals, birds, were entirely different from those they were accustomed to, on the other side of the great waters. They travelled and travelled, till they wore out all of the clothing that had been given to them, and had to take to their leather clothing again.

The three days the chief spoke of meant three years, for it was only at the end of the third year that they came within the sound of the spirit's rattle. The sound appeared to be near, but they continued walking on, day after day, without apparently getting any nearer to it. Suddenly they came to a very extensive plain. They could see the blue ridges of distant mountains rising on the horizon beyond it. They pushed on, thinking to get over the plain before night, but they were overtaken by darkness. They were now on a stony part of the plain, covered by about a foot's depth of water. They were weary and fatigued.

Some of them said, 'Let us lie down.'

'No, no,' said the others, 'let us push on.'

Soon they stood on firm ground, but it was as much as they could do to stand, for they were very weary. They, however, made an effort to encamp, lighted a fire and refreshed themselves by eating. They then began conversing about the sound of the spirit's rattle, which they had heard for several days. Suddenly the noise began again; it sounded as if it was subterraneous, and it shook the ground. They tied up their bundles and went towards the spot. They soon came to a large building which was illuminated. As soon as they came to the door, they were met by a rather elderly man.

'How do ye do,' said he, 'my grandsons? Walk in, walk in; I am glad to see you; I knew when you started; I saw you encamp this evening. Sit down and tell me the news of the country you left, for I am interested in it.'

They complied with his wishes, and when they had concluded, each one presented him with a piece of tobacco. He then revealed to them things that would happen in their journey, and predicted its successful accomplishment.

'I do not say that all of you,' said he, 'will successfully go through it. You have passed over three-fourths of your way, and I will tell you how to proceed after you get to the edge of the earth. Soon after you leave this place, you will hear a deafening sound. It is the sky descending on the edge, but it keeps moving up and down. You will watch, and when it moves up, you will see a vacant space between it and the earth. You must not be afraid. A chasm of awful depth is there, which separates the unknown from this earth, and a veil of darkness conceals it. Fear not. You must leap through; and if you succeed, you will find yourselves on a beautiful plain, and in a soft and mild light emitted by the moon.'

They thanked him for his advice. A pause ensued.

'I have told you the way,' he said. 'Now tell me again of the country you have left, for I committed dreadful ravages while I was there. Does not the country show marks of it? And do not the inhabitants tell of me to their children? I came to this place to mourn over my bad actions and am trying, by my present course of life, to relieve my mind of the load that is on it.'

They told him that their fathers spoke often of a celebrated personage called Manabozho, who performed great exploits.

'I am he,' said the spirit. They gazed with astonishment and fear.

'Do you see this pointed house?' said he, pointing to one that resembled a sugar loaf. 'You can now each speak your wishes, and will be answered from that house. Speak out, and ask what each wants, and it shall be granted.'

One of them, who was vain, asked with presumption that he might live for ever, and never be in want. He was answered, 'Your wish shall be granted.' The second made the same request, and received the same answer. The third asked to live longer than common people, and to be always successful in his war excursions, never losing any of his young men. He was told, 'Your wishes are granted.' The fourth joined in the same request, and received the same reply. The fifth made a humble request, asking to live as long as men generally do, and that he might be crowned with such success in hunting as to be able to provide for his parents and relatives. The sixth made the same request, and it was granted to both, in pleasing tones, from the pointed house.

After hearing these responses they prepared to depart. They were told by Manabozho that they had been with him but one day, but they afterward found that they had remained there upward of a year.

When they were on the point of setting out, Manabozho exclaimed, 'Stop! You two, who asked me for eternal life, will receive the boon you wish immediately.' He spoke, and one was turned into a stone called Shin-gauba-wossin and the other into a cedar tree.

'Now,' said he to the others, 'you can go.'

The moon was happy to see them; she informed them that they were halfway to her brother's and that from the earth to her abode was half the distance.

They left him in fear, saying, 'We were fortunate to escape so, for the king told us he was wicked, and that we should not probably escape from him.' They had not proceeded far when they began to hear the sound of the beating sky. It appeared to be near at hand, but they had a long interval to travel before they came near, and the sound was then stunning to their senses; for when the sky came down, its pressure would force gusts of wind from the opening, so strong that it was with difficulty they could keep their feet, and the sun passed but a short distance above their heads. They, however, approached boldly, but had to wait some time before they could muster courage enough to leap through the dark veil that covered the pas-

sage. The sky would come down with violence, but it would rise slowly and grad-ually.

The two who had made the humble request stood near the edge, and with no little exertion succeeded, one after the other, in leaping through, and gaining a firm foothold. The remaining two were fearful and undecided. The others spoke to them through the darkness, saying, 'Leap! Leap! The sky is on its way down.' These two looked up and saw it descending, but fear paralysed their efforts; they made but a feeble attempt, so as to reach the opposite side with their hands. But the sky at the same time struck the earth with great violence and a terrible sound, and forced them into the dreadful black chasm.

The two successful adventurers, of whom Isoco now was chief, found them-selves in a beautiful country, lighted by the moon, which shed around a mild and pleasant light. They could see the moon approaching as if it were from behind a hill. They advanced, and an aged woman spoke to them; she had a white face and pleas-ing air, and looked rather old, though she spoke to them very kindly. They knew from her first appearance that she was the moon. She asked them several ques-tions; she told them that she knew of their coming, and was happy to see them; she informed them that they were half-way to her brother's, and that from the earth to her abode was half the distance.

'I will, by and by, have leisure,' said she, 'and will go and conduct you to my brother, for he is now absent on his daily course. You will succeed in your object, and return in safety to your country and friends, with the good wishes, I am sure, of my brother.'

While the travellers were with her, they received every attention. When the proper time arrived, she said to them, 'My brother is now rising from below, and we shall see his light as he comes over the distant edge. Come,' said she, 'I will lead you up.' They went forward, but in some mysterious way they hardly knew how; they rode almost directly up, as if they had ascended steps. They then came upon an immense plain, declining in the direction of the sun's approach. When he came near, the moon spoke, 'I have brought you these persons, whom we knew were coming,' and with this she disappeared. The sun motioned with his hand for them to follow him. They did so, but found it rather difficult, as the way was steep. They found it particularly so from the edge of the earth till they got half-way between that point and midday.

When they reached this spot the sun stopped and sat down to rest.

'What, my children,' said he, 'has brought you here? I could not speak to you before. I could not stop at any place but this, for this is my first resting place; then at the centre, which is at midday, and then half-way from that to the western edge. Tell me,' he continued, 'the object of your undertaking this journey and all the cir-cumstances which have happened to you on the way.'

They complied. Iosco told him their main object was to see him. They had lost four of their friends on the way, and they wished to know whether they could return in safety to the earth, that they might inform their friends and relatives of all that had befallen them. They concluded by requesting him to grant their wish-es. He replied, 'Yes, you shall certainly return in safety; but your companions were vain and presumptuous in their demands. They were Foolish Ones. They aspired to what Manitous only could enjoy. But you two, as I said, shall get back to your country and become as happy as the hunter's life can make you. You shall never be in want of the necessaries of life as long as you are permitted to live; and you will have the satisfaction of relating your journey to your friends, and also of telling them of me. Follow me, follow me,' he said, commencing his course again.

The ascent was now gradual, and they soon came to a level plain. After travelling some time he again sat down to rest, for he had arrived at the half-way line.

'You see,' said he, 'it is level at this place, but a short distance onward, my way descends gradually to my last resting place, for which there is an abrupt descent.' He repeated his assurance that they should be shielded from danger if they relied firmly on his power.

'Come here quickly,' he said, placing something before them on which they could descend. 'Keep firm,' said he, as they resumed the descent. They went downwards as if they had been let down by ropes.

In the meantime, the parents of these two young men dreamed that their sons were returning, and that they should soon see them. They placed the fullest confidence in their dreams. Early in the morning they left their lodges for a remote point in the forest, where they expected to meet them. They were not long at the place before they saw the adventurers returning, for they had descended not far from that place. The young men knew they were their fathers. They met and were happy. They related all that had befallen them. They did not conceal anything; and they expressed their gratitude to the different Manitous who had preserved them, by feasting and gifts, and particularly to the sun and moon, who had received them as their children.

Mon-daw-min, or the Origin of Indian Corn

Chippewa and Ojibwa

IN TIMES PAST, a poor Indian was living with his wife and children in a beautiful part of the country. He was not only poor but was not expert in procuring food for his family, and his children were all too young to give him assistance. Although poor, he was a man of a kind and contented disposition. He was always thankful to the Great Spirit for everything he received.

The same disposition was inherited by his eldest son, who had now arrived at the proper age to undertake the ceremony of the Ke-ig-uish-im-o-win, a fast to see what kind of spirit would be his guide and guardian through life. Wunzh, for this was his name, had been an obedient boy from his infancy, and was of a pensive, thoughtful and mild disposition, so that he was beloved by the whole family. As soon as the first indications of spring appeared, they built him the customary little lodge at a retired spot, some distance from their own, where he would not be disturbed during this solemn rite. In the meantime, he prepared himself, and immediately went into it and commenced his fast.

The first few days, he amused himself in the mornings by walking in the woods and over the mountains, examining the early plants and flowers, and in this way prepared himself to enjoy his sleep, and at the same time stored his mind with pleasant ideas for his dreams. While he rambled through the woods, he felt a strong desire to know how the plants, herbs and berries grew without any aid from man,

Source
Henry R. Schoolcraft, *North American Indian Legends,* Philadelphia: J.B. Lippincott & Co., 1856, p. 99

and why it was that some species were good to eat and others possessed medicinal or poisonous juices. He recalled these thoughts to mind after he became too languid to walk about and had confined himself strictly to the lodge. He wished he could dream of something that would prove a benefit to his father and family, and to all others.

'True,' he thought, 'the Great Spirit made all things, and it is to him that we owe our lives. But could he not make it easier for us to get our food than by hunting animals and taking fish? I must try to find this out in my visions.'

On the third day he became weak and faint, and kept to his bed. He fancied, while thus lying, that he saw a handsome young man coming down from the sky and advancing towards him. He was richly and gaily dressed, having on a great many garments of green and yellow colours, but differing in their deeper or lighter shades. He had a plume of waving feathers on his head, and all his motions were graceful.

'I am sent to you, my friend,' said the celestial visitor, 'by that Great Spirit who made all things in the sky and on the earth. He has seen and knows your motives in fasting. He sees that it is from a kind and benevolent wish to do good to your people, and to procure a benefit for them, and that you do not seek for strength in war or the praise of warriors. I am sent to instruct you, and show you how you can do your kindred good.' He then told the young man to arise, and prepare to wrestle with him, as it was only by this means that he could hope to succeed in his wishes.

Wunzh knew he was weak from fasting, but he felt his courage rising in his heart, and immediately got up, determined to die rather than fail. He commenced the trial and, after a protracted effort, was almost exhausted, when the beautiful stranger said, 'My friend, it is enough for once; I will come again to try you'; and smiling on him, he ascended in the air in the same direction from which he came.

The next day the celestial visitor reappeared at the same hour and renewed the trial. Wunzh felt that his strength was even less than the day before, but the courage of his mind seemed to increase in proportion as his body became weaker. Seeing this, the stranger again spoke to him in the same words he used before, adding, 'Tomorrow will be your last trial. Be strong, my friend, for this is the only way you can overcome me, and obtain the boon you seek.'

On the third day he again appeared at the same time and renewed the struggle. The poor youth was very faint in body, but grew stronger in mind at every contest, and was determined to prevail or perish in the attempt. He exerted his utmost powers, and after the contest had been continued the usual time, the stranger ceased his efforts and declared himself conquered. For the first time he entered the lodge and, sitting down beside the youth, he began to deliver his instructions to him, telling him in what manner he should proceed to take advantage of his victory.

The Celestial Visitor told the young man to arise and prepare to wrestle with him.

'You have won your desires of the Great Spirit,' said the stranger. 'You have wrestled manfully. Tomorrow will be the seventh day of your fasting. Your father will give you food to strengthen you, and as it is the last day of trial, you will prevail. I know this, and now tell you what you must do to benefit your family and your tribe. Tomorrow I shall meet you and wrestle with you for the last time; and as soon as you have prevailed against me, you will strip off my garments and throw me down, clean the earth of roots and weeds, make it soft and bury me in the spot.

When you have done this, leave my body in the earth, and do not disturb it, but come occasionally to visit the place to see whether I have come to life, and be careful never to let the grass or weeds grow on my grave. Once a month cover me with fresh earth. If you follow my instructions, you will accomplish your object of doing good to your fellow creatures by teaching them the knowledge I now teach you.' He then shook him by the hand and disappeared.

In the morning, the youth's father came with some light refreshments, saying, 'My son, you have fasted long enough. If the Great Spirit will favour you, he will do it now. It is seven days since you have tasted food and you must not sacrifice your life. The Master of Life does not require that.'

'My father,' replied the youth, 'wait till the sun goes down. I have a particular reason for extending my fast to that hour.'

'Very well,' said the old man, 'I shall wait till the hour arrives and you feel inclined to eat.'

At the usual hour of the day, the sky visitor returned and the trial of strength was renewed. Although the youth had not availed himself of his father's offer of food, he felt that new strength had been given to him, and that exertion had renewed his strength and fortified his courage. He grasped his angelic antagonist with supernatural strength, threw him down, took from him his beautiful garments and plume and, finding him dead, immediately buried him on the spot, taking all the precautions he had been told of, and being very confident, at the same time, that his friend would again come to life.

He then returned to his father's lodge and partook sparingly of the meal that had been prepared for him. But he never for a moment forgot the grave of his friend. He carefully visited it throughout the spring, and weeded out the grass, and kept the ground in a soft and pliant state. Very soon he saw the tops of the green plumes coming through the ground; and the more careful he was to obey his instructions in keeping the ground in order the faster they grew. He was, however, careful to conceal the exploit from his father. Days and weeks had passed in this way.

The summer was now drawing towards a close, when one day, after a long absence in hunting, Wunzh invited his father to follow him to the quiet and lonesome spot of his former fast. The lodge had been removed, and the weeds kept from growing on the circle where it stood, but in its place stood a tall and graceful plant, with bright-coloured silken hair, surmounted with nodding plumes and stately leaves, and golden clusters on each side.

'It is my friend,' shouted the lad. 'It is the friend of all mankind. It is Mon-daw-min. We need no longer rely on hunting alone, for as long as this gift of corn is cherished and taken care of, the ground itself will give us a living.'

He then pulled an ear. 'See, my father,' said he, 'this is what I fasted for. The Great Spirit has listened to my voice, and sent us something new, and henceforth our people will not alone depend upon the chase or upon the waters.'

He then told his father the instructions given him by the stranger. He told him that the broad husks must be torn away, as he had pulled off the garments in his wrestling. And having done this, directed him how the ear must be held before the fire till the outer skin became brown, while all the milk was retained in the grain. The whole family then united in a feast on the newly grown ears, expressing gratitude to the Merciful Spirit who gave it. So corn came into the world.

SHE WHO HAS A SOUL

Great Lakes Sioux

IT WAS A LONG TIME AGO, nearly two hundred years ago, that some of our people were living upon the shores of the Great Lake, Lake Superior. The chief of this band was called Tatankaota, Many Buffaloes.

One day the young son of Tatankaota led a war-party against the Ojibways, who occupied the country east of us, towards the rising sun. When they had gone a day's journey in the direction of Sault St Marie, in our language Skesketatanka, the warriors took up their position on the lake shore, at a point which the Ojibways were accustomed to pass in their canoes.

Long they gazed, and scanned the surface of the water, watching for the coming of the foe. The sun had risen above the dark pines, over the great ridge of woodland across the bay. It was the awakening of all living things. The birds were singing and shining fishes leaped out of the water as if at play. At last, far off, there came the warning cry of the loon to stir their expectant ears.

'Warriors, look close to the horizon! This brother of ours does not lie. The enemy comes!' exclaimed their leader. Presently upon the sparkling face of the water there appeared a moving canoe. There was but one, and it was coming directly towards them.

'Hahatonwan! Hahatonwan!' they exclaimed with one voice, and, grasping their weapons, they hastily concealed themselves in the bushes. 'Spare none – take no captives!' ordered the chief's son.

Nearer and nearer approached the strange canoe. The glistening blades of its paddles flashed as if it were the signal of good news or a welcome challenge. All impatiently waited until it should come within arrow-shot.

'Surely it is an Ojibway canoe,' one murmured. 'Yet look! The stroke is ungainly!' Now, among all the tribes only the Ojibway's art is perfect in paddling a birch canoe. This was a powerful stroke, but harsh and unsteady.

'See! There are no feathers on this man's head!' exclaimed the son of the chief. 'Hold, warriors, he wears a woman's dress, and I can see no weapon. No courage is needed to take his life, and therefore let it be spared! I command that only coups (blows) be counted on him, and he shall tell us from where he comes, and on what errand.'

The signal was given; the warriors sprang to their feet, and like wolves they sped from the forest, out upon the white, sandy beach and straight into the sparkling waters of the lake, giving the shrill war-cry, the warning of death! The solitary oarsman made no outcry – he offered no defence! Kneeling calmly in the prow of the little vessel, he merely ceased paddling and seemed to await with patience the deadly blow of the tomahawk.

The son of Tatankaota was foremost in the charge, but suddenly an impulse seized him to stop his warriors, lest one in the heat of excitement should do a mischief to the stranger. The canoe with its occupant was now very near, and it could be seen that the expression of his face was very gentle and even benignant. None could doubt his utter harmlessness; and the chief's son afterwards declared that at this moment he felt a premonition of some event, but whether good or evil he could not tell.

Source

Charles A. Eastman, (Ohiyesa). *Old Indian Days*, New York: McClure Company, 1907, pp. 208–18

No blows were struck – no coups counted. The young man bade his warriors take up the canoe and carry it to the shore; and although they murmured somewhat among themselves, they did as he commanded them. They seized the light bark and bore it dripping to a hill covered with tall pines and overlooking the waters of the Great Lake.

Then the warriors lifted their war-clubs over their heads and sang, standing around the canoe in which the black-robed stranger was still kneeling. Looking at him closely, they perceived that he was of a peculiar complexion, pale and inclined to red. He wore a necklace of beads, from which hung a cross bearing the form of a man. His garments were strange, and most like the robes of woman. All of these things perplexed them greatly.

Presently the Black Robe told them by signs, in response to their inquiries, that he came from the rising sun, even beyond the Great Salt Water, and he seemed to say that he formerly came from the sky. Upon this the warriors believed that he must be a prophet or mysterious man.

Their leader directed them to take up again the canoe with the man in it, and appointed the warriors to carry it by turns until they should reach his father's village. This was done according to the ancient custom, as a mark of respect and honour. They took it up forthwith, and travelled with all convenient speed along the lake shore, through forests and across streams to a place called the Maiden's Retreat, a short distance from the village.

Thence the chief's son sent a messenger to announce to his father that he was bringing home a stranger, and to ask whether or not he should be allowed to enter the village.

'His appearance,' declared the scout, 'is unlike that of any man we have ever seen and his ways are mysterious!'

When the chief heard these words, he immediately called his council-men together to decide what was to be done, for he feared by admitting the mysterious stranger to bring some disaster upon his people. Finally he went out with his wisest men to meet his son's war-party. They looked with astonishment upon the Black Robe.

'Dispatch him! Dispatch him! Show him no mercy!' cried some of the council-men.

'Let him go on his way unharmed. Trouble him not,' advised others.

'It is well known that the evil spirits sometimes take the form of a man or animal. From his strange appearance I judge this to be such a one. He should be put to death, least some harm befall our people,' an old man urged.

By this time several of the women of the village had reached the spot. Among them was She Who Has a Soul, the chief's youngest daughter, whom tradition says was a maiden of much beauty, and of a generous heart. The stranger was evidently footsore from much travel and weakened by fasting. When she saw that the poor man clasped his hands and looked skyward as he uttered words in an unknown tongue, she pleaded with her father that a stranger who has entered their midst unchallenged may claim the hospitality of the people, according to the ancient custom.

'Father, he is weary and in want of food. Hold him no longer! Delay your council until he is refreshed!' These were the words of She Who Has a Soul, and her father could not refuse her prayer. The Black Robe was released, and the Sioux maiden led him to her father's tepee.

She anointed the blistered feet of the holy man with perfumed otter oil.

Now the warriors had been surprised and indeed displeased to find him dressed after the fashion of a woman, and they looked upon him with suspicion. But from the moment that she first beheld him, the heart of the maiden had turned towards this strange and seemingly unfortunate man. It appeared to her that great reverence and meekness were in his face, and with it all she was struck by his utter fearlessness, his apparent unconsciousness of danger.

The chief's daughter, having gained her father's permission, invited the Black Robe to his great buffalo-skin tent and, spreading a fine robe, she gently asked him to be seated. With the aid of her mother, she prepared wild rice sweetened with maple sugar and some broiled venison for his food. The youthful warriors were astonished to observe these attentions, but the maiden heeded them not. She anointed the blistered feet of the holy man with perfumed otter oil, and put upon him a pair of moccasins beautifully worked by her own hands.

It was only an act of charity on her part, but the young men were displeased, and again urged that the stranger should at once be turned away. Some even suggested harsher measures; but they were overruled by the chief, softened by the persuasions of a well-beloved daughter.

During the few days that the Black Robe remained in the Sioux village he preached earnestly to the maiden, for she had been permitted to converse with him by signs, that she might try to ascertain what manner of man he was. He told her of the coming of a 'Great Prophet' from the sky, and of his words that he had left with the people. The cross with the figure of a man he explained as his totem which he had told them to carry. He also said that those who love him are commanded to go among strange peoples to tell the news, and that all who believe must be marked with holy water and accept the totem.

He asked by signs if She Who Has a Soul believed the story. To this she replied, 'It is a sweet story – a likely legend! I do believe!'

Then the good father took out a small cross and, having pressed it to his heart and crossed his forehead and breast, he gave it to her. Finally he dipped his finger in water and touched the forehead of the maiden, repeating meanwhile some words in an unknown tongue.

The mother was troubled, for she feared that the stranger was trying to bewitch her daughter, but the chief decided thus: 'This is a praying-man, and he is not of our people; his customs are different, but they are not evil. Warriors, take him back to the spot where you saw him first! It is my desire, and the good custom of our tribe requires that you free him without injury!'

Accordingly they formed a large party, and carried the Black Robe in his canoe back to the shore of the Great Lake, to the place where they had met him, and he was allowed to depart thence and go wherever he chose. He took his leave with signs of gratitude for their hospitality, and especially for the kindness of the beautiful Sioux maiden. She seemed to have understood his mission better than anyone else, and as long as she lived she kept his queer trinket – as it seemed to the others – and performed the strange acts that he had taught her.

Furthermore, it was through the pleadings of She Who Has a Soul that the chief Tatankaota advised his people in after days to befriend the white strangers, and though many of the other chiefs opposed him in this, his counsel prevailed. Hence it was that both the French and the English received much kindness from our people, mainly through the influence of this one woman!

Such was the first coming of the white man among us, as it is told in our traditions. Other praying-men came later, and many of the Sioux allowed themselves to be baptized. True, there have been Indian wars, but not without reason; and it is pleasant to remember that the Sioux were hospitable to the first white 'praying-man', and that it was a tender-hearted maiden of my people who first took in her hands the cross of the new religion.

STORIES OF WAK-CHUNG-KAKA AND WASH-CHING-GEKA
Winnebago

MA-O-NA, THE EARTH-MAKER, made the earth and everything on it. He made a man, but the man was not good. Ma-o-na did not want to burn him up, so he tossed him to one side and went on with his work. This man became Wa-cho-pi-ni-shi-shik, an evil spirit. He watched Ma-o-na at work, and everything that Ma-o-na made he copied; but whereas Ma-o-na's works were all good, those of Wa-cho-pi-ni-shi-shik were evil. Ma-o-na made the deer and elk and buffalo; Wa-cho-pi-ni-shi-shik made the huge animals, the monsters that devoured men. All bad things, evil spirits and the like, are the work of Wa-cho-pi-ni-shi-shik.

Ma-o-na sent his son, Wak-chung-kaka, the Foolish One, to kill the monsters and make the earth fit for man. But Wak-chung-kaka could not destroy all the works of the evil spirit. Then Ma-o-na sent another son, Ke-chung-geka, the Tortoise, but he was too fond of war. So, too, was Wuh-te-huk, the third son. Last of all Ma-o-na sent his youngest son, Wash-ching-geka, the Little Hare.

These are stories of Wak-chung-kaka and Wash-ching-geka.

STORIES OF WAK-CHUNG-KAKA, THE FOOLISH ONE

I

One day Wak-chung-kaka was walking over a hill and he looked down into a hollow where reeds grew tall, and he thought he saw a throng of people with feathers on their heads. The wind blew through the reeds, and Wak-chung-kaka thought that the people danced and hallooed, 'Wu-wu-wu!' So he put a feather on his head and went in among the people and danced and shouted, 'Wu-wu-wu!' He danced all day long, till at evening the wind dropped and everything was still; and then Wak-chung-kaka looked around him and found himself alone among the reeds.

II

Wak-chung-kaka was walking one day beside the water when he saw a chief standing there dressed all in black with a shining disc on his breast, and the chief was pointing across the water. He stood quite still, and always pointed steadily across the water. Wak-chung-kaka spoke to him, but the chief never moved or answered; he still pointed steadily across the water. Wak-chung-kaka spoke to him again, and still there was no answer. Four times he spoke to him, and then at last Wak-chung-kaka grew angry and said, 'I can point too, and I can point longer than you.'

Source
Natalie Curtis
Burlin, *The
Indians' Book*,
New York:
Harper and
Brothers, 1923,
pp. 244–50

So Wak-chung-kaka set down his bundle and opened it and dressed himself all in black like the chief, and hung a disc on his breast and stood there beside the chief, pointing across the water. But when he had stood thus for a great time without moving, Wak-chung-kaka began to be weary of this, and he looked around at the chief, and, behold, it was only the blackened stump of a burned tree with a white spot that the fire had not touched.

III

Another time Wak-chung-kaka was walking along the sandy shore of a lake, and when he came to a point of the shore he heard a cry, 'Wu-wu-wu!' He looked over the point, but could see nobody, so he walked on till he heard the cry, 'Wu-wu-wu!' and saw a little cloud of flies fly up into the air. There was an elk's head lying on the shore, and a swarm of flies flew in at the neck-hole behind, and then flew out again all at once. Wak-chung-kaka stood and looked at them. 'That must be good sport,' he thought. 'I wish I could do that too.'

A little fly looked up at him and said, 'Wak-chung-kaka, you can!'

At once Wak-chung-kaka felt himself growing smaller and smaller, till he was no bigger than a fly, and then he easily went in at the hole in the head and flew out again, crying, 'Wu-wu-wu!' He thought it was fine sport to fly in and out, in and out, with the swarm of flies. So the flies let him play with them for a while, till all at once, when Wak-chung-kaka was just starting to go in, he grew to his own natural size, and as he already had his head within the elk's head, the neck-hole fitted him so closely that he could not get his head out again.

Wak-chung-kaka walked on, wearing the elk's head; and as he could not see very well, he walked into the lake. The water came up to the eye-holes of the head, and Wak-chung-kaka swam until he came near to a village that stood beside the lake, and when the people saw the elk-horns moving along the water they said, 'It is a water-spirit; let us offer him gifts.' For there are spirits in the ground, under the water, and in the great springs of the hills, and the spirits often look like elk or buffalo.

So the people brought tobacco and beads and laid them on the shore before Wak-chung-kaka, and he stayed in the water; and the young people prayed to him, 'Spirit, grant us long life!' and the old people prayed, 'Long life for our children!' and to every prayer Wak-chung-kaka answered, 'Ho! (yes)'. At length, when all the people were gathered before him, he said, 'My nephews and nieces, I will grant your prayers if you will do what I tell you. Let two strong men take hold of my horns, one on each side, and let another one split my head down the middle, carefully, carefully – he must be careful not to cut too deep.'

So two strong men took hold of his horns, one on each side, and pulled with all their might, while the third took a stone axe and very carefully chopped the elk's head down the middle, till, crack, the skull fell apart and there stood Wak-chung-kaka, and laughed, 'Haw, haw, haw!'

Wak-chung-kaka stayed in the water and the young people prayed to him, 'Spirit, grant us long life!'

STORIES OF WASH-CHING-GEKA, THE LITTLE HARE

I

Wash-ching-geka lived with his grandmother while he was doing his works. His grandmother was the earth, and she was very wise. She cooked for the Little Hare and nourished him and took care of him.

Now among the other evil things then in the world were eight blind men who lived in a wood; they went about with the help of long cords and spread webs among the trees, in which they caught people and killed them.

One day when the blind men were cooking their dinner of bear's meat, Wash-ching-geka went in among them. There was a piece of meat for each. Now the men could not see Wash-ching-geka, and he stepped softly to the pot and took out one portion of meat. When the blind men began to eat they quarrelled with one another over the missing portion, because each one thought another had taken his meat. As they were quarrelling, Wash-ching-geka slapped one of them, and then that one slapped his neighbour, and he slapped the next, and so they all fell to fighting.

Meanwhile, Wash-ching-geka ran home to his wise grandmother and took counsel with her.

Next day he went again to the blind men, and while they were cooking he took out the meat and put poison on it. So the blind men ate of the poisoned meat and were killed. They would never again spread webs among the trees to destroy the people. And now when they were dead, behold, Wash-ching-geka saw that really they were spiders.

II

In the early days there was a great hill that used to open and shut like a pair of jaws and devour men and animals. The hill would open in the middle and the sides would fall back till they lay flat upon the ground, and all the land looked like good smooth prairie.

Then herds of elk and deer and buffalo would come to graze, and when the place was full, the jaws of the hill would close and, crack, all the animals would be crushed and killed. This hill killed so much game that the Earth-maker feared that all the people would starve. So he sent his son, Wash-ching-geka, to destroy the hill.

When the Little Hare came there the hill opened and all the ground was smooth; and Wash-ching-geka made himself like a small stone and lay quite still. Then the elk and deer and buffalo came to graze, but as soon as the mouth began to close on them, see, Wash-ching-geka quickly changed himself into a great stone, and so, when the hill shut on him, hoo, the jaws were broken all to pieces. The hill lay shattered and never could devour men or animals any more.

MANABOZHO

Algonquin

A RED MOON RODE the windy sky. A great, dark, bat-like shadow screened it for the length of a heartbeat. An owl hooted eerily in the depth of the dark forest; then the shrill shrieks of a newborn man-child filled the air. All night noises ceased. Black clouds veiled the moon, and the sky was filled with the wings of many birds in wild flight. Forest animals fled in terror. Manabozho, transformer and trickster, had been born. Very little is told of his early boyhood. We take him up in the following legend at a period of advanced youth, when we find him living with his grandmother. And at this time he possessed, although he had not yet exercised, all the anomalous and contradictory powers of body and mind, of manship and divinity, which he afterwards evinced.

The timidity and rawness of the boy quickly gave way in the courageous developments of the man. He soon evinced the sagacity, cunning, perseverance and heroic courage which constitute the admiration of the Indians. And he relied largely upon these in the gratification of an ambitious, vainglorious and mischief-loving disposition. In wisdom and energy he was superior to anyone who had ever lived before. Yet he was simple when circumstances required it, and was ever the object of tricks and ridicule in others. He could transform himself into any animal he pleased, being man or Manito, as circumstances rendered necessary. He often conversed with animals, fowls, reptiles and fish. He deemed himself related to them, and invariably addressed them by the term 'my brother'; and one of his greatest resources, when hard-pressed, was to change himself into their shapes.

◆

Manabozho was living with his grandmother near the edge of a wide prairie. On this prairie he first saw animals and birds of every kind. He there also saw exhibitions of divine power in the seeping tempests, in the thunder and lightning, and the various shades of light and darkness, which form a never-ending scene of observation. Every new sight he beheld in the heavens was a subject of remark; every new animal or bird an object of deep interest; and every sound uttered by the animal creation a new lesson, which he was expected to learn. He often trembled at what he heard and saw.

To this scene his grandmother sent him at an early age to watch. The first sound he heard was that of the owl, at which he was greatly terrified, and quickly descending the tree he had climbed, he ran with alarm to the lodge. 'Noko! Noko!' he cried, 'I have heard a monedo (evil spirit).' She laughed at his fears, and asked him what kind of noise it made. He answered, 'It makes a noise like this, Ko-ko-ko-ho.' She told him that he was young and foolish, that what he had heard was only a bird, deriving its name from the noise it made.

He went back and continued his watch. While there, he thought to himself, 'It is singular that I am so simple, and my grandmother so wise, and that I have neither father nor mother. I have never heard a word about them. I must ask and find out.' He went home and sat down silent and dejected.

At length his grandmother asked him, 'Manabozho, what is the matter with you?'

Source
Henry R. Schoolcraft, *North American Indian Legends*, Philadelphia: J.B. Lippincott & Co., 1856, pp. 33–47

He answered, 'I wish you would tell me whether I have any parents living, and who my relatives are.' Knowing that he was of a wicked and revengeful disposition, she dreaded telling him the story of his parentage, but he insisted on her compliance.

'Yes,' she said, 'you have a father and three brothers living. Your mother is dead. She was taken without the consent of her parents by your father, the West. Your brothers are the North, the East and the South, and being older than yourself, your father has given them great power with the winds, according to their names. You are the youngest of his children. I have nourished you from your infancy, for your mother died in giving you birth, owing to the ill-treatment of your father. I have no relations besides you this side of the planet in which I was born, and from which I was precipitated by female jealousy. Your mother was my only child, and you are my only hope.'

He appeared to be rejoiced to hear that his father was living, for he had already thought in his heart to try and kill him. He told his grandmother he should set out in the morning to visit him. She said it was a long distance to the place where Ningabiun, wind of the West, lived. But that did not stop him, for he had now attained manhood, possessed a giant's height, and was endowed by nature with a giant's strength and power. He set out and soon reached the place, for every step he took covered a large surface of ground. The meeting took place on a high mountain in the west. His father was very happy to see him. He also appeared pleased. They spent some days in talking with each other.

One evening Manabozho asked his father what he was most afraid of on earth. He replied, 'Nothing.'

'But is there not something you dread here? Tell me.'

At last his father said, yielding, 'Yes, there is a black stone found in such a place. It is the only thing earthly I am afraid of; for if it should hit me or any part of my body, it would injure me very much.'

He said this as a secret, and in return asked his son the same question. Knowing each other's power, although the son's was limited, the father feared him on account of his great strength. Manabozho answered, 'Nothing!' intending to avoid the question, or to refer to some harmless object as the one of which he was afraid. He was asked again and again, and answered, 'Nothing!' But the West said, 'There must be something you are afraid of.'

'Well! I will tell you,' said Manabozho, 'what it is.'

But before he would pronounce the word, he affected great pain. '*Ie-ee – Ie-ee –* it is – it is,' said he. '*Yeo! Yeo!* I cannot name it; I am seized with a dread.'

The West told him to banish his fears. He commenced again, in a strain of mock sensitiveness, repeating the same words. At last he cried out, 'It is the root of the bulrush.' He appeared to be exhausted by the effort of pronouncing the word, in all this skilfully acting a studied part.

Some time after he observed, 'I will get some of the black rock.'

The West said, 'Far be it from you; do not do so, my son.' He still persisted.

'Well,' said the father, 'I will also get the *apukwa* root.' Manabozho immediately cried out, 'No! No!' affecting, as before, to be in great dread of it, but really wishing, by this course, to urge on the West to procure it, that he might draw him into combat. He went out and got a large piece of the black rock and brought it home. The West also took care to bring the dreaded root.

In the course of conversation, he asked his father whether he had been the cause of his mother's death. The answer was, 'Yes!' He then took up the rock and struck him. Blow led to blow, and here commenced an obstinate and furious combat, which continued several days. Fragments of the rock, broken off under Manabozho's blows, can be seen in various places to this day. The root did not prove as mortal a weapon as his well-acted fears had led his father to expect, although he suffered severely from the blows. This battle commenced on the mountains. The West was forced to give ground. Manabozho drove him across rivers, and over mountains and lakes, and at last he came to the brink of this world.

'Hold!' cried he. 'My son, you know my power, and that it is impossible to kill me. Desist, and I will also portion you out with as much power as your brothers. The four quarters of the globe are already occupied; but you can go forth and do a great deal of good to the people of this earth, which is infested with large serpents, beasts and monsters, who make great havoc among the inhabitants. Go and do good. You have the power now to do so, and your fame with the beings of this earth will last for ever. When you have finished your work, I will have a place provided for you. You will then go and sit with your brother Kabibboonocca in the north.'

Manabozho was pacified. He returned to his lodge, where he was confined by the wounds he had received. But from his grandmother's skill in medicines he was soon recovered.

◆

Some time after this he commenced making preparations for a war excursion against the Pearl Feather, the Manitou who lived on the opposite side of the great lake, who had killed his grandfather. The abode of this spirit was defended, first, by fiery serpents, who hissed fire so that no one could pass them; and, second, by a large mass of gummy matter lying on the water, so soft and adhesive that whoever attempted to pass, or whatever came in contact with it, was sure to stick there.

He continued making bows and arrows without number, but he had no heads for his arrows. At last Noko told him that an old man who lived at some distance could make them. He sent her to get some. She soon returned with her *conaus*, her wrapper, full. Still he told her he had not enough, and sent her again. She returned with as much more. He thought to himself, 'I must find out the way of making these heads.' Cunning and curiosity prompted him to make the discovery. But he deemed it necessary to deceive his grandmother in so doing.

'Noko,' said he, 'while I take my drum and rattle, and sing my war-songs, go and try to get me some larger heads for my arrows, for those you brought me are all of the same size. Go and see whether the old man cannot make some a little larger.'

He followed her as she went, keeping at a distance, and saw the old artificer at work, and so discovered his process. He also beheld the old man's daughter, and perceived that she was very beautiful. He felt his breast beat with a new emotion, but said nothing. He took care to get home before his grandmother, and commenced singing as if he had never left his lodge. When the old woman came near, she heard his drum and rattle, without any suspicion that he had followed her. She delivered him the arrowheads.

One evening the old woman said, 'My son, you ought to fast before you go to war, as your brothers frequently do, to find out whether you will be successful.' He said he had no objection, and immediately commenced a fast for several days. He would retire every day from the lodge so far as to be out of reach of his grandmother's voice. It seems she had indicated this spot, and was very anxious he should fast there, and not at another place. She had a secret motive, which she carefully hid from him. Deception always begets suspicion. After a while he thought to himself, 'I must find out why my grandmother is so anxious for me to fast at this spot.'

Next evening he went but a short distance. She cried out, 'A little farther off'; but he came nearer to the lodge, and called in a low voice, to make it appear that he was distant. She then replied, 'That is far enough.' He had got so near that he could see all that passed in the lodge. He had not been long in his place of concealment, when a man in the shape of a bear entered the lodge. He had very long hair. They commenced talking about him, and appeared to be improperly familiar. At that time people lived to a very great age, and he perceived, from the marked attentions of this visitor, that he did not think a grandmother too old to be pleased with such attentions.

He listened to their conversation some time. At last he determined to play on the visitor a trick. He took some fire and, when the bear had turned his back, touched his long hair. When the animal felt the flame, he jumped out, but the open air only made it burn the fiercer, and he was seen running off in a full blaze.

Manabozho ran to his customary place of fasting and, assuming a tone of simplicity, began to cry out, 'Noko! Noko! Is it time for me to come home?'

'Yes,' she cried. When he came in, she told him what had taken place, at which he appeared to be very much surprised.

After having finished his term of fasting and sung his war-song – from which the Indians of the present day derive the custom – he embarked in his canoe, fully prepared for war. In addition to the usual implements, he had a plentiful supply of oil. He travelled rapidly night and day, for he had only to will or speak, and the canoe went. At length he arrived in sight of the fiery serpents. He stopped to view them. He saw they were some distance apart, and that only the flame which issued from them reached across the water. He commenced talking as a friend to them; but they answered, 'We know you, Manabozho, you cannot pass.'

He then thought of some expedient to deceive them, and hit upon this. He pushed his canoe as near as possible. All at once he cried out, with a loud and terrified voice, 'What is that behind you?' The serpents instantly turned their heads, when, at a single word, he passed them.

'Well,' said he placidly, after he had got by, 'how do you like my exploit?' He then took up his bow and arrows, and with deliberate aim shot them, which was easily done, for the serpents were stationary and could not move beyond a certain spot. They were of enormous length and of a bright colour.

Having overcome the sentinel serpents, he went on in his magic canoe till he came to a soft gummy portion of the lake, called Pigiu-wagumee, Pitchwater. He took the oil and rubbed it on his canoe, and then pushed into it. The oil softened the surface and enabled him to slip through it with ease, although it required frequent rubbing and a constant reapplication of the oil. Just as his oil failed, he extricated himself, and was the first person who ever succeeded in overcoming it.

He now came in view of land, on which he disembarked in safety, and could see the lodge of the Shining Manitou, situated on a hill. He commenced preparing for the fight, putting his arrows and clubs in order, and just at the dawn of day began his attack, yelling and shouting, and crying with triple voices, 'Surround him! Surround him! Run up! Run up!' making it appear that he had many followers. He advanced, crying out, 'It was you that killed my grandfather,' and with this shot his arrows.

The combat continued all day. Manabozho's arrows had no effect, for his antagonist was clothed with pure wampum. He was now reduced to three arrows, and it was only by extraordinary agility that he could escape the blows which the Manitou kept making at him. At that moment a large woodpecker, the *ma-ma*, flew past, and alighted on a tree.

'Manabozho,' he cried, 'your adversary has a vulnerable point; shoot at the lock of hair on the crown of his head.' He shot his first arrow so as only to draw blood from that part. The Manitou made one or two unsteady steps, but recovered himself. He began to parley, but in the act received a second arrow, which brought him to his knees. But he again recovered. In so doing, however, he exposed his head, and gave his adversary a chance to fire his third arrow, which penetrated deep, and brought him, a lifeless corpse, to the ground.

Manabozho uttered his *saw-saw-quan*, his war-cry, and, taking the scalp as a trophy, he called the woodpecker to come and receive a reward for his information. He took the blood of the Manitou and rubbed it on the woodpecker's head, the feathers of which are red to this day.

After this victory he returned home, singing songs of triumph and beating his drum. When his grandmother heard him, she came to the shore and welcomed him with songs and dancing. Glory fired his mind. He displayed the trophies he had brought in the most conspicuous manner, and felt an unconquerable desire for other adventures. He felt himself urged by the consciousness of his power to new trials of bravery, skill and necromantic prowess. He had destroyed the Manitou of Wealth, and killed his guardian serpents and eluded all his charms.

PART 4
THE GREAT PLAINS

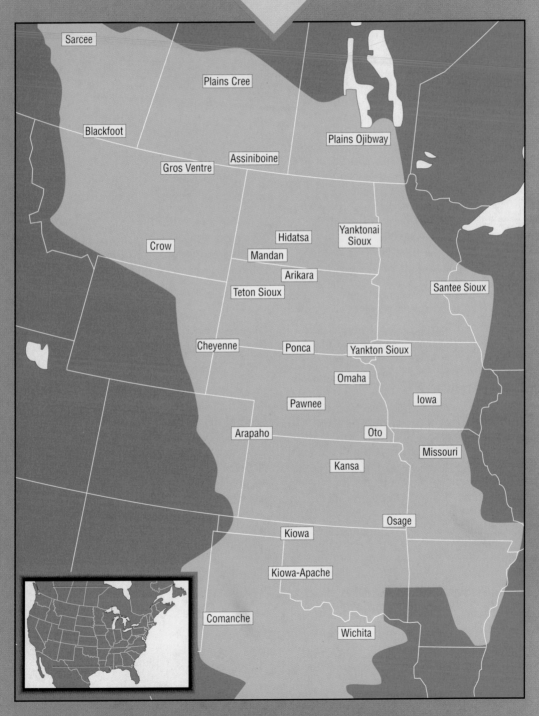

Sarcee

Plains Cree

Blackfoot

Plains Ojibway

Gros Ventre

Assiniboine

Crow

Hidatsa

Yanktonai Sioux

Mandan

Arikara

Santee Sioux

Teton Sioux

Cheyenne

Ponca

Yankton Sioux

Omaha

Iowa

Pawnee

Arapaho

Oto

Missouri

Kansa

Osage

Kiowa

Kiowa-Apache

Comanche

Wichita

TRIBES OF THE GREAT PLAINS

The tribes of the Great Plains have become, thanks to the influence of Hollywood and countless television series, the North American cultural group that most people can call to mind. Generations of films, from the Howard Hawks–John Wayne cavalry epics, such as *She Wore a Yellow Ribbon*, to Arthur Penn's *Little Big Man* and Kevin Costner's *Dances with Wolves*, have presented the Plains tribes as the quintessential Indian groups of history, as well as cinematography. Conical tepees with their hide coverings, 'peace pipes', war bonnets of eagle feathers, fiercely painted warriors on their swift ponies, bows or rifles at the ready, chasing down lumbering buffalo: these are the typical images of the Native Americans of North America. Even our stock image of warfare between Native Americans and whites is generated from one battle between Plains tribes such as the Sioux and Northern Cheyenne and units of nineteenth-century US cavalry led by their flamboyant yet flawed commander, George Armstrong Custer: the Battle of the Little Bighorn.

While such images are potent and pervasive, they do not give a clear picture of life among the tribes of the Great Plains, much less an accurate view of Native Americans across the continent. And, perhaps ironically, the main elements of nineteenth-century Plains Indian culture – assumed to be the horse and the rifle – were not Native American in their origins but were derived from contact with white culture. In addition, the days of the Great Plains tribes' 'horse and buffalo' culture were, in the greater span of Indian history, relatively short lived, lasting about 150 years, depending on the tribe's first access to horses.

The history of the Native Americans of the Great Plains predates the arrival of Europeans on the North American continent by several thousand years During those centuries, eastern Plains peoples lived in relatively permanent villages and practised a rudimentary agriculture, with food from hunting being supplementary at best.

The Great Plains Region

The area of the Great Plains stretches across the borders of two nations today: the United States and Canada. From the vast, empty grasslands of Alberta, Manitoba and Saskatchewan to the southern brush lands of Texas, the Great Plains include all or portions of over a dozen states. The Mississippi River marks the region's furthest eastern edge, generally along the 97th meridian, while the foothills of the Rocky Mountains rise above the flatlands, serving as the boundary to the west. With little variation, the Plains form a steppe that rises gradually from east to west. There are breaks and disturbances in the landscape, however, including the Ozark Mountains of southern Missouri and northern Arkansas, the Wichita Mountains of Oklahoma and the Black Hills of South Dakota.

Average annual rainfall divides the Great Plains into two subregions, roughly along the 100th meridian, which runs north and south, bisecting the Dakotas and Nebraska, and separates the western thirds of Kansas, Oklahoma and Texas from their eastern parts. East of the line, the average rainfall is from twenty to forty inches (fifty to one hundred centimetres), while to the west the average precipitation is from ten to twenty inches (twenty five to fifty centimetres). Until recently, archaeologists and historians assumed that before the introduction of the horse North American tribes did not occupy the Plains, especially the drier western areas. However, it is now thought that the Plains have been inhabited for more than 11,000 years. Prehistoric studies reveal that nomadic groups occupied nearly all of the region between 10,000 and 7,000 years ago. These Neolithic groups hunted mammoths and bison. Then, between 7,000 and 4,500 years ago, the Plains groups nearly abandoned the region, due to a warming trend. The great Pleistocene animals left the area, and those people who remained were reduced to living on small game and gathering wild plants and berries.

About 4,500 years ago, the Great Plains experienced a repopulation. Many of those who found their way out on to the Plains came from the eastern woodlands. The resulting Plains Woodland period was firmly entrenched in the region between 500 BC and AD 1000. Between AD 200 and 400, a stable, semi-permanent village life existed in eastern Kansas, Nebraska, Colorado, northeastern Oklahoma and along the course of the Missouri River. Here, bands of Native Americans planted corn and beans for food, as well as relying on the hunt and gathering wild plants. Grave sites from this period reveal a culture that produced pottery, used tools and weapons of stone and bone and worked small amounts of copper into artefacts.

By AD 800, a generalized movement of bands from the woodlands east of the Mississippi River developed, bringing new settlements and villages to the eastern Plains. These peoples often built their villages along major rivers and streams. They raised the crops known as the Three Sisters – corn, beans and squash – as well as sunflowers. These Plains village bands constructed square or rectangular earthen lodges or mud-covered huts, which were often surrounded by protective palisades. Hunting was important to these tribes, with the men fanning out in search of bison, while the women did the farming, using digging sticks and hoes made from bison scapulae.

Around the year 1500 many of these farming–hunting villages of the western Plains were abandoned, probably as a result of drought. About this time, Plains cultural groups, separated from one another by hundreds of miles of empty, treeless land, began to move about, making contact with one another. Through interaction, the tribes of the northern and southern Plains developed a new culture, with larger villages and a greater reliance on agriculture. These new villages were increasingly permanent, leading to a more sedentary life. The earthen lodges were altered, becoming circular, for reasons that are not currently understood.

By the time the Europeans arrived on the Great Plains in the sixteenth and seventeenth centuries, several distinct subcultures were in place, located throughout the region. Scattered along the lower Missouri River basin were the Iowas, Kansas, Missouris, Omahas, Osages, Otos and Poncas. The Arikaras, Hidatsas and Mandans lived near the middle course of the Missouri River. To the south, across the modern-day state of Missouri, were the Pawnees. And south of them were the Wichitas. Each of these tribal groups lived in agricultural villages.

In all, twenty-six tribal groups have been identified by anthropologists as the nations of the Plains. They include those tribes mentioned above, plus the following: Sarcee, Blackfoot, Cree, Ojibway, Gros Ventre, Assiniboine, Crow, Shoshone, Arapaho, Cheyenne, Kiowa, Kiowa-Apache, Comanche and the wide-ranging group called the Sioux, also known as the Dakota or Lakota.

Great Plains Horse Culture

Once the peoples of the Plains experienced contact with the European explorers, trappers, traders and missionaries of the seventeenth and eighteenth centuries, they began to alter their culture. Perhaps no other regional group of Native Americans prior to 1800 was changed as much by white contact as the Plains tribes. Southwestern tribes were using the horse by the 1680s and 1690s. By 1750, most Plains tribes had horses, which had originally been brought by the Spanish in the 1500s. With the incorporation of the horse into their culture, Plains Indian groups came to rely less on systematic agriculture for their primary sources of food. By the eighteenth century, these tribes were developing the horse and buffalo culture by which they have come to be recognized. The horse provided hunters with greater mobility, allowing them to range considerable distances from their band's village in search of buffalo. Some tribes, particularly in the northern reaches of the Plains, were late or even slow to adopt the horse, and here farming remained paramount in the provision of food.

With the introduction of the horse, Plains tribes became, just as their ancestors hundreds of years before them, nomadic once again.

At the same time that Plains tribes were gaining access to the horse, other groups were being pushed on to the Plains by the ever-moving whites. Soon the Plains became populated by new tribes who had migrated from lands east of the Mississippi. Among them were the Arapaho, Cheyenne, Cree, Crow, Gros Ventre, Kiowa, Kiowa-Apache, Ojibway and Sioux. An extraordinary interaction developed between these tribes. They shared and adopted one another's customs, both new and old. They exchanged practices related to agriculture, horseback buffalo-hunting, methods of war and the newly developed shelter of lodge poles and buffalo-hide coverings called tepees. They also developed a hand-sign language in order to facilitate trade and communication between the leaders of different tribes.

While Plains dwellers identified themselves through tribal membership, their most immediate connection was to their individual band. Bands were made up of several families, both related and unrelated, with each generally boasting, at best, several hundred persons. Bands tended to live apart from one another throughout most of the year, but would come together during the summer months for joint buffalo hunts and religious rituals and ceremonies.

The Horse and Buffalo

Without a doubt, the adoption of the horse by the Native Americans of the Plains dramatically altered their culture, their means of transportation and their tribal economies. The horse – called Sacred Dog by some Plains tribes; Medicine Dog or Spirit Dog by others – became, in time, a symbol of wealth among the tribes.

These powerful animals were used in many ways by Plains tribes. Not only did they provide mobility for distant buffalo hunts, they also became a primary means of transport. Before the arrival of the horse on the North American continent, tribes relied on the dog as their beast of burden. They would attach two small poles, lashed together in a V-shape, to the dog's back, then stretch an animal hide between the poles to provide a carrier for the tribe's material goods. This device, called a travois, was small and limited by the dog's capacity to pull the dead weight behind it. With the coming of the horse, Plains Indians built larger travois that could carry greater weights, including ill or wounded adult men and women.

Great Plains peoples became very adept horsemen. Often they rode their animals bareback, using only one leather strap as a bridle. They rode their mounts skilfully into battle against neighbouring tribes, learning how to cling to a horse's flanks, protecting themselves from arrows and rifle balls. Sometimes they would fire their weapons from beneath their horse's neck.

Horses became important symbols for the Plains dwellers signifying wealth to fellow tribesmen. The more horses a warrior owned, the greater his status in the tribe. While most male tribal members owned fewer than ten horses, some warriors, especially tribal chiefs, might own hundreds and even as many as 1,000. Horses were used as a medium of exchange, usually having a value relative to buffalo robes, guns, steel knives and other Western trade goods. When a man chose a wife, he gave her family horses as a dowry. One tribe would often raid the horse reserves of a neighbouring tribe, adding the stolen animals to their own inventory. Stealing a horse was considered an act of bravery, skill and cunning.

Tribesmen decorated their horses in various ways, using paint, feathers and beadwork. Although most rode without the benefit of a saddle, some warriors fashioned small saddles of buffalo hide. Sometimes they might make wooden saddles sheathed in deer or antelope skin, decorating them with intricate patterns of beadwork. They also painted their ponies with their own personal symbols. Others decorated their steeds by dipping the ponies' tails in paint. Warriors took their small yet powerfully swift ponies into battle on more than one occasion against each other and against units of the US army, where they usually outmanoeuvred the larger army mounts.

If the horse eventually became the Plains tribes' source of wealth, transport, warfare and mobility, the buffalo became their primary source of meat and other necessities. Before the adoption of the horse, Plains tribes could hunt only for buffalo that were located near a tribe's village. Warriors usually attempted to run a buffalo herd off a nearby cliff or into a ravine, where their quarry would either die from the fall or be trapped, allowing hunters to kill them with their arrows or rifles. Running a herd off a cliff usually resulted in great waste, as more buffalo died than the band of hunters could butcher and consume.

Once they began relying on the horse for mobility and speed in hunting, Plains tribes became equally dependent on the buffalo for food, clothing and shelter. Tribesmen prepared the animal's meat in a variety of ways, but usually roasted strips of flesh or ate them raw. Most tribes enjoyed the buffalo's hump and considered its meat to be quite tender. They also drank buffalo blood, which, it is said, has the taste of warm milk, and unborn calf foetus was considered a delicacy. They ate the buffalo's organs, including the intestines, and even the animal's bone marrow. Buffalo meat was also preserved for future meals, as well. Since refrigeration was non-existent in those days on the Plains, they cut buffalo meat into long strips and hung them over wooden frames to dry in the sun, creating jerky. To provide a ready food source in the winter when buffalo hunting was difficult or impossible, tribal women prepared a substance called pemmican. Pemmican was a mixture of pulverized buffalo meat, animal fat and wild berries. Once these foods were combined, the pemmican was placed in leather pouches and often buried. During snowy months, they would dig up their bags of stored food and were thus able to keep themselves alive thanks to forward planning.

Plains tribes not only utilized the buffalo meat but attempted to use nearly every other part of the animal in one way or another. They developed nearly a hundred uses for the parts of a buffalo, including robes, tepee coverings, shields and leather pouches, called parfleches. Women worked buffalo hides by scraping away the flesh and softening the animal covering into leather by applying ashes, animal fat and brains, and plant fibres. Tools were fashioned from the animal's bones. Thread for sewing clothing, as well as for stringing bows, was made from buffalo sinew. Ceremonial rattles were made from buffalo hoofs and horns. Skulls were used in Indian rituals as well. Even the dung of the buffalo, so-called 'buffalo chips', was used as fuel for campfires when trees and wood were not available in adequate quantities.

Plains Tepees

While not every Plains tribe lived in conical-shaped dwellings of wooden poles and buffalo hides called tepees, this means of shelter was typically used right across the Great Plains region. Generally, the men of a tribe were responsible for gathering the materials required to build a tepee. However, it was considered women's work to put a tepee together, to maintain the dwelling once erected, and to dismantle and transport it when the tribe moved to another site.

Most tepees followed the same basic construction design. Three or four poles were lashed together near their ends and placed upright to form the simple support structure. Other poles were then placed among them, forming a circle on the ground.

These poles provided the framework for the house. Women sewed buffalo hides together, the number of hides determined by the desired size of the tepee. Smaller tepees required as few as six or seven buffalo hides, while larger structures demanded up to twenty or thirty. Larger tepees indicated greater wealth and status for a warrior among his peers. Once the hides were stretched around the lodge pole framework, the women used wooden stakes, or lodge pins, to secure the hide to the ground all around the base. Lodge poles placed inside the tepee were used to open and close flaps located at the top of the structure. Such flaps could be opened to allow smoke to escape from the inside or closed to block out rain or snow. A buffalo hide was used as a door covering for the entrance. Generally, peoples on the Plains built their tepees with entrances facing out to the east, since the winds of the Plains often blow from the west. Plains tepees could be both cool in summer and warm in winter.

To the Plains tribes, such lodgings were not just places to live in. They were decorated with paintings of spirits, deceased ancestors and records of deeds carried out in battle. The tepee provided a series of symbols for Plains tribes. The rounded shape of the dwelling represented the interconnectedness of all parts of life. Most tepees featured an altar stone where warriors prayed while incense burned on the stone.

Earthen Lodges of the Mandan

Nearly every Plains tribe had come to live in tepees by the eighteenth century. A few, however, did not. One such northern Plains tribe was the Mandans. These people migrated on to the Plains around 1400 from the Great Lakes region and settled along the Missouri River in territory that is today North Dakota. When whites first made contact with the Mandans in the 1700s, they were living in the Big Bend region of the Missouri River.

The Mandans lived in permanent settlements and practised an extensive agriculture, which included the raising of corn, beans, squash, sunflowers and tobacco for ceremonial purposes. They built their homes in the form of earthen mounds rather than relying on the tepee design. To construct a typical Mandan dwelling involved digging a pit measuring one to four feet (thirty to 120 centimetres) in depth. This provided the floor for the lodge. A wooden frame was built up from the pit floor, with the poles lashed together and covered with several layers of willow branches, followed by a layer of prairie grass to provide insulation. Sod was then placed on top of the willow branches and grasses to provide the roof of the dwelling. These earthen houses had to provide warmth for the Mandan during the long winter months with temperatures far below freezing. The average Mandan village might feature from ten to a hundred earthen lodges.

These rounded lodges served as home to several families who lived together and often numbered as many as forty or fifty, if not more. Each family provided its own beds, which were placed around the wall of the lodge circle. In the centre of the lodge, a fire burned, providing warmth for the occupants and heat for cooking. In the centre of the lodge's roof, a hole allowed the fire's smoke to escape.

The Mandans were not the only northern Plains tribes to use the earthen lodge as a residence. In all, eight groups lived for at least for a majority of the year in such dwellings: in addition to the Mandan, these were the Arikaras, the Hidatsas, the Pawnees, the Omahas, the Caddos, the Wichitas and the Osages.

Plains Clothing

As with most people who live in temperate zones, the typical wardrobe of a Plains dweller varied according to the season. In summer, the men of the tribe wore leather breechclouts. The women wore sleeveless leather dresses. Both men and women wore moccasins. Children often went naked in summer, as well as barefoot. In winter, everyone wrapped themselves in buffalo robes, leggings and animal-skin shirts. The clothing of both men and women was frequently decorated with porcupine quills and beads.

Warriors wore their hair in a variety of styles and sported several different types of head-dresses. Typically, braves wore eagle feathers attached directly to their hair. As they participated in battles and raids, warriors accumulated many honours, resulting in a head-dress brimming with eagle's feathers. These elaborate headpieces might include feathers, their tips dipped in black paint, which were attached to the skullcap of a buffalo, along with headbands embellished with fur, porcupine quills, beads and painted ribbons.

As to hairstyles, there was great variation. The men of some tribes shaved their heads entirely or left a centre strip of hair running to the back of the head, which might then be ornamented with a colourful fringe of stiffened deer-tail hair. Others left their hair unshorn, with a single forelock falling across the forehead. Regardless, nearly all warriors used feathers further to adorn their hairstyles.

Village Life

Within most Plains tribes, there were few authoritarian structures in place to govern the conduct of the tribe or its bands. Most bands operated independently of one another, selecting their own chiefs. Such men were chosen on the basis of their military successes, their leadership qualities and their perceived wisdom. Such men rarely gave strict orders to their people but were, rather, advisers. Discipline for each band often took the form of shunning members, shaming them or even forcing them out of the band.

When a tribe's bands came together, as they often did in summer, each band set up camp by erecting their tepees in a circle. Such villages, then, took on the shape of a series of circles adjacent to one another. At such times competitions were often held between bands, such as foot or horse races or gambling sessions. Certainly the bands shared the experiences of prescribed ceremonies, festivals and councils.

While life on the Plains for Native Americans could be filled with daily diversions, excitements and adventures, village life was often a matter of routine and pattern, generally determined by the passing of the seasons. Tribes people typically referred to their years as 'winters', indicating their awareness of seasonal differences. When winter approached, indicated by the first snowfall, the Plains tribes often carried out one last hunt, hoping to add to their stores of meat from the spring and summer forays. As the snows came and the temperatures dropped, village life for all members became sedentary. Often the camps established by the various bands of a tribe in November became permanent until the arrival of spring in early May.

A Plains winter could be a ferocious experience. Snows were often measured in feet rather than inches on the northern Plains and temperatures dropped sixty or seventy degrees Fahrenheit below freezing. Buffalo-hide tepees did, however, generally provide adequate warmth inside. Sleeping at night was done under small heaps of buffalo furs, with family members lying close to one another for warmth. Although winterbound, everyone had jobs to do. Men worked at repairing their hunting equipment, restringing bows and shaping new arrows. Women cooked and tended the children, as well as decorating hides and articles of clothing with beadwork and porcupine quills. Children had their own tasks to do, although they also spent much time playing games, often indoors. In the evenings, families came together to share stories and meals. Around a dancing fire, old men spun tales, young men and women paired off with one another, and children drifted off to sleep under heavy buffalo robes.

Despite the cold outdoor temperatures, activity did continue during winter camp beyond the warm interior of the tepees. Fighting between tribes was rare in winter, yet intrepid warriors did attempt an occasional horse-stealing raid against their neighbours. Braves patrolled their own encampments, always on the watch for the warriors of other tribes. If food stocks dwindled, small hunting parties might be sent out to try to replenish or supplement them.

With the long-awaited arrival of spring, the bands emerged from their relatively dormant lifestyle, ready for a move and new adventure. Springtime activities included the bands coming together for important ceremonies, such as those associated with planting, especially for the sedentary tribes. New chiefs might be selected, and a plan was laid out to determine each band's new encampment site.

Throughout much of the later spring and most of the summer, the nomadic tribal bands and clans scattered in all directions, becoming largely responsible for themselves. They each moved to a designated vicinity, yet they were free to move about at will and as often as they chose. Each band established its own pattern of hunting, warring and horse-stealing. By midsummer, the separated bands came together for the annual Sun Dance, the most significant series of annual ceremonies each tribe engaged in. Following the Sun Dance rituals, most Plains tribes engaged in a great buffalo hunt.

By autumn, the sedentary tribes began to reap the harvest of their agricultural endeavours, while nomadic bands continued to hunt, bartering with one another and dealing with white traders, and to work on their domestic and decorative crafts.

Plains Warfare

War was common among Plains tribes, as it would be in the nineteenth century between Native Americans and white soldiers and settlers. Plains warfare featured practices that were unique to the tribal culture. The warriors of many tribes belonged to military societies, typically entering them upon reaching a certain age, generally during their teen years. Such societies imposed a specific code of behaviour on their members and required specific dances, songs and insignia.

Some societies were intertribal, meaning their members could come from different tribes, although these were rare. Others were more closed, membership being 'by invitation only'. Invitation often hinged on the warrior's personal record of exploits and deeds in battle. One of the greatest acts of bravery a Plains warrior could carry out was the curious practice of 'counting coup'.

While most cultures who wage war expect their fighting men to kill the enemy, the Plains Indians had a custom of humiliating an enemy by merely touching him and perhaps allowing him to live. In such instances, a warrior carried a 'coup' stick into a skirmish, using it to tap or touch his opponent. (The word *coup* is French, meaning 'blow'.) Counting coup was not limited to such official sticks, and using a bow, a lance, a club or even a hand was perfectly acceptable. A brave usually received an eagle feather for each successful coup. A coup might then be followed by a killing, then a scalping. All three acts committed together resulted in the warrior receiving three eagle feathers. Such acts of bravery, the mere touching of an armed opponent, were often recounted later around tribal fires, as warriors told of their exploits of the day and of days past. Warriors often embellished their stories, but any brave caught exaggerating his deeds might face the permanent shame of his fellow tribesmen.

Plains Religion

To the typical Native American of the Great Plains, the spirit world was a potent place, one that was interconnected with the natural world in which they found themselves. Their religion, as was true of all tribes in the Americas, was by nature animistic. All things – plants, animals, the stars and planets, water, even rocks – had spirits whose qualities could, at least in part, be passed on to warriors who performed certain deeds.

For many Great Plains tribes a practice called the 'vision quest' became an important avenue for making connection between the natural and the spirit world. Warriors sought visions through an involved series of rituals. A brave usually

attempted his first vision quest as a teenager. Normally, the process began with the building of a sweat lodge from tree saplings, something similar to a sauna, with the warrior sitting inside. Stones were heated inside the lodge and steam was created by pouring water over the hot rocks. This process 'purified' the brave. He then stripped off his clothing, painted his body with white clay and secluded himself outside the camp, fasting for several days.

After days without food and water, plus continuous exposure to the elements, the warrior hoped to receive a vision – actually an induced hallucination. These visions were considered a window to the spirit world. If such a vision did not occur, the brave might then cut himself repeatedly, the resulting loss of blood often causing him to become semi-conscious, thus creating a trance-like state.

Once the vision came, it took on a variety of possible forms. The hallucinating brave might receive a visit from a deceased ancestor or have a conversation with an animal. Some visions involved rainstorms, visits to places unknown to the dreamer or a long list of other natural phenomena. During the course of the vision, the brave hoped to learn sacred songs and prayers, and receive instruction on behaviour. Once the vision had taken place, the warrior then often related his dream to a medicine man who would serve as the vision's interpreter. Whatever was considered to be the vision's most potent symbol – an animal, a tree or a natural element – was thought to be that warrior's guardian spirit. The brave then began collecting objects that he recalled from his vision to serve as charms. These were then placed in a sacred pouch called a medicine bundle.

Medicine Bundles

These leather pouches were considered powerful medicine to the Plains people who carried them. They included not only objects remembered from visions but other items considered sacred by members of the tribe. Medicine bundles were thought to possess magical powers and brought good fortune to the warrior and his family. While individuals usually carried their own medicine bundles, many Plains bands had medicine bundles of their own. Such bundles were held by tribal chiefs, medicine men or shamans, and their contents were considered sacred to the entire band or even to the whole tribe. Sacred items, such as smoking pipes, were often found among the potent inventory of tribal medicine bundles.

Sacred Pipes

Pipes were used in many of the sacred and ceremonial rituals of the Great Plains tribes. They were considered holy, sacred and spiritually powerful. Individuals often made their own pipes, but many bands and tribes had pipes that belonged to the entire group. Most pipes were made of wood, sometimes with the stem extending several feet in length. Other pipes were fashioned out of a soft, reddish rock called catlinite. The most famous catlinite quarry, located in Minnesota, was itself considered sacred, and braves from many different tribes came there. No warfare was to take place on this holy ground and enemies worked within sight of one another, carving out pieces of catlinite to fashion into pipe bowls and stems. Other Plains pipes were fashioned out of steatite, or soapstone. These were typically decorated with porcupine quills, feathers, beads and horsehair.

The tribes considered these pipes to be sacred, partly because of the tobacco burned in them, which was itself considered sacred. Although the common term used by Europeans for such pipes is 'peace pipes', these sacred objects were not used in peace councils. For those occasions, any pipe would do. Sacred pipes, on the other hand, served as the symbolic protection for the tribe, guarding the welfare and security of its people, whether an individual family, a band or the entire tribe.

The Sacred Sun Dance

While some vision quests were individually directed, the result of a lone warrior seeking his personal directive, most Plains tribes carried out a highly symbolic annual event, which was called by the Sioux the Sun Dance. While it went by other names – New Life Lodge among the Cheyennes; Mystery Dance among the Poncas –

the Sun Dance served as a yearly attempt by each tribe to make connection with the spiritual world.

Such connection was believed to be necessary for the good fortune of the tribe. It was needed to keep the buffalo abundant, to bring prosperity to the tribe, to bless marriages, to heal sick members and to ensure the renewing cycles of nature, such as the sun continuing its course through the sky each day.

The Sun Dance, and all its associated, peripheral activities, was held in the summertime, when a tribe's bands had joined together for extensive buffalo-hunting. Many special events took place, including horse races and interband competitions. Chief among the important events were the teaching of holy songs and the selection of a warrior to cut a tree for the sacred pole to serve as the centrepiece of the Sun Dance. Band chiefs met in councils to renew acquaintances, tell stories and re-create tribal unity. The apex of all this interaction was, however, the Sun Dance itself. It began during a full moon, usually in late summer, when the wild chokeberries were ripe for picking. The ceremony accompanying the Sun Dance lasted from eight to twelve days.

While the many rituals making up the Sun Dance were very involved, each one being highly symbolic, the dance itself took place around the freshly cut and painted pole, which had been carved out of a sacred tree trunk. Such poles were often as much as thirty feet (nine metres) in height. A wall was often raised around the pole, creating a sacred lodge. Those who danced around the pole did so in a simple repeated series of steps, which continued for days, with the participants denying themselves food and water. Just as with individual vision quests, these Sun Dance warriors were working themselves into a trance, in search of a vision.

Other Sun Dance rituals included a process of self-mutilation. Taking a knife, braves cut slits in their chests and ran wooden skewers through their skin. Rawhide straps were attached to the skewers, connected to the sacred pole. While drums beat out an endless rhythm, warriors danced back away from the pole, until the skewers ripped from their flesh. Other braves danced around with their skewers attached to bison skulls, dragging the skulls behind them. These self-mutilation exercises were designed to induce hallucination, and individual sacrifice was thought to bring good fortune to the entire tribe.

Mythology of the Plains Tribes

The Plains tribes as other Native Americans, believed in a supreme being, a rather vaguely defined presence called the Sky Father who was the guardian of all. Between his home in the sky and the earth below, Plains mythology continued, was a middle place, the home of not only distant planets, stars, the sun and moon, but beings closer to earth, such as eagles, clouds, lightning and thunder. Their lives between the sky and the earth were lived in much the same way as the tribes themselves lived: in tepees and earthen-lodge dwellings. These spirits frequently visited the earth and could take on human form, and could wreak havoc by causing droughts or floods, or making the buffalo herds disappear. Alternatively, they could bless individual warriors, as well as bands and whole tribes. Plains Indians believed that such spiritual beings could be appeased through self-mutilation and pain. This explains the importance of the Sun Dance rituals and individual vision quests.

Creation Myths of the Plains

Several different stories existed among the tribes of the Plains to explain the origins of the earth and how men and women came to be created. One such myth, as told by the Arikaras, related man's origins from beneath the earth's surface. In this myth, two ducks are enticed by two creatures named Wolf Man and Lucky Man to dive into a giant lake and retrieve mud from which the earth was fashioned. Once that was done, Wolf Man and Lucky Man went beneath the earth and convinced two spiders to give birth to a variety of animals and a race of giants.

Watching all this from his sky perch, the great Sky Spirit, Nesaru (the Sioux Indians gave him the name Wakonda), disliked the giants, because they did not worship him. In retaliation, he created corn. From the seeds of the corn,

Nesaru created a race of human beings similar to the tribes people themselves. He then sent the Corn Mother down to earth to fetch the newly created people to the surface. Once she appeared underground, the Corn Mother was soon surrounded by the people and their animals. Several animals began burrowing towards the earth's surface – the badger, the mole and the mouse – but the hole they created was not big enough. Thunder shook the earth and loosened the soil, allowing the Corn Mother, the humans and the animals to emerge on the earth's surface.

Once they found themselves on the earth rather than under it, the human beings were directed by various birds – the kingfisher, the owl and the loon – to the places where they should live. In time, the humans began to fight and quarrel with one another. Nesaru and the Corn Mother finally appeared and each taught the humans everything they needed to know about planting and growing corn, about the gods of the sky, how to live at peace with one another and, when war became necessary, how to fight with honour. The Corn Mother explained to the human beings the magical properties of medicine bundles and the good fortune that they represented.

Before Nesaru and the Corn Mother left the humans, disease arrived, delivered by the Wind of the Southeast, one of the Gods of the Eight Directions of the Sky. To help the people, a dog appeared and it told them how to cure diseases and gave them medicine. As Nesaru prepared to leave, he left his personal medicine bundle with the humans, and the Corn Mother gave them a cedar tree as a symbol of her constantly present spirit. The two gods then ascended into the sky.

Myth of the Morning Star

A myth such as the preceding one places much emphasis on the power of the gods in the sky and of medicine bundles. Some Plains groups considered the gods in the heavens so important to their tribal mythology that they had tribal sky-watchers, men who served as astronomers, tracking the movements of the planets and the phases of the moon. They often decided when were the best times of the year to make offerings and to carry out sacred ceremonies. Such tribes recognized and worshipped the North Star, considering it to be the god of creation, identifying the South Star as a dark force, in command of the beings of the underworld. The star they called the Morning Star provided them with tribal comfort and security. The Evening Star was a dark power who sent his own daughter to diminish the powers of the Morning Star.

To ensure the continuation of the Morning Star in the sky, Plains tribes created a medicine bundle called the Morning Star bundle. A legend was developed and a ritual carried out every four years. A tribe's braves raided a neighbouring camp and kidnapped a young girl. After holding her prisoner and giving her messages for the gods in the sky, the braves stripped her naked and painted her half red and half black, these two colours symbolizing the Morning and Evening Stars. The young prisoner was then tied to a platform where the tribe's warriors killed her, shooting her body full of arrows. This human sacrifice and the shedding of her blood were intended as an offering to the Sky Father, who would then bless the tribe for another four years.

MYTHS AND LEGENDS OF THE GREAT PLAINS

THE MADNESS OF BALD EAGLE

Sioux

'IT WAS MANY YEARS AGO, when I was only a child,' began White Ghost, the patri-archal old chief of the Yankton Sioux, 'that our band fought a hard battle with the Rees and the Mandans. The reason for the fight was an odd one. I will tell you the story'. And he laid aside his long-stemmed pipe and settled in for the telling.

'At that time the Yankton numbered a little over forty families. We were nick-named by the other bands Shunkikcheka, or Domestic Dogs, because of our own-ing large numbers of these animals. My father was the head chief.

'Our favourite wintering place was a tract of timberland near the mouth of the Grand River (the Missouri), and it was here that we met with the Blackfoot Sioux for the annual fall hunt. Across the river, on the opposite bank, was the permanent village of the Rees and Mandans, whose houses were built partially underground of dirt and poles. For a hundred years before this time, they had planted great gar-dens, and we often traded them for corn, beans and pumpkins. Our peoples occa-sionally made treaties of peace between one another. Each Ree family had one or two buffalo boats – made from two or three skins – not rounded, as the Sioux made them. They carried their dried beans and other vegetables to us in these boats, and we traded buffalo meat jerky with them.

'It was a great time of celebration and hospitality. The Sioux braves were court-ing the Ree girls, and the Ree young men were courting the girls of our band. Meanwhile, the older people were busy trading with one another. It was a time of joy as the river came alive with canoes, trade and the laughter of the young men and maidens.

Bald Eagle pulled out his gun and shot the Ree dead.

'My uncle – my father's younger brother – whose name was Big Whip, had a close friend named Bald Eagle. Both men were known for their ambition and dar-ing. They had been following the Ree girls to their canoes each evening.

'Big Whip and his friend stood on the river's bank at sunset, one with a quiver full of arrows on his back while the other carried a gun underneath his blanket. Nearly all the village's people had crossed the river and the Ree chief, whose name was Bald Eagle, went home with his wife after everyone else was gone. It was about dusk as they entered their bull-hide boat. The two Sioux braves stood there watch-ing them.

'Suddenly Big Whip exclaimed, 'Friend, let us kill the chief. I dare you to scalp him!'

'His friend answered, 'It shall be as you ask. I will stand by you through this and will die with you.'

Source

Charles A. Eastman, (Ohiyesa). *Old Indian Days*, New York: McClure Company, 1907, pp. 68–75

'Then Bald Eagle pulled out his gun and shot the Ree dead. From that day on he took his name. The old chief fell back into his boat, and his wife screamed and cried as she rowed him across the river. The other young man shot an arrow or two at her, but she continued to row until she arrived on the opposite bank.

'There was great excitement on both sides of the river as soon as the people found out what had happened. There were two camps of Sioux, the Blackfoot Sioux and the Yankton, or our people. Naturally, the Mandans and Rees greatly outnumbered us. Their camp must have numbered at least two or three thousand, which was more than we had between our two camps put together.

'There was a Sioux whose name was Black Shield, who had a Ree wife. He came down to the river bank and shouted to us, "Of which one of your bands is the man who killed Bald Eagle?"

'One of the Blackfoot Sioux replied, "It is a man of the Yankton Sioux who killed Bald Eagle."

'Then he said, "The Rees desire to battle with the Yanktons. You had better separate from their camp."

'Accordingly the Blackfeet retired about a mile from our camp, upon the bluffs, and pitched their tents, while the Yankton remained on the prairie. The two bands had been great rivals in the practice of war, so we did not ask for help from them, but during the night we dug two trenches around our camp, the outer one for the men to battle and the inner one to provide protection for the women and children.

'The next morning at dawn the enemy crossed the river and approached our camp in great numbers. Some of their old men and women also came to watch the battle from the bluffs. The Blackfeet also came to watch from the bluffs. Just before the battle began, one Blackfoot came into our camp along with his wife. He intended to fight alongside us. His name was Red Dog's Track, but after that day, he was called He Came Back. His wife was a Yankton and he had told her, "If I don't join your tribe today, my brothers-in-law will call me a coward."

'The Sioux were well entrenched and well armed with both guns and bows and arrows. Their aim was so deadly that the Rees crawled towards them slowly and picked off any Sioux who tried to show his head above the trenches. Similarly, every Ree who exposed himself was certain to die.

'Up to this time no one had seen the two braves responsible for this battle. There was a natural hollow in the river bank which was concealed by buffalo berry bushes, close to the spot where they stood when Bald Eagle shot the Ree.

'"Friend," said Big Whip, "It is likely that our own people will punish us for our deeds. They will hunt us down and punish us for our crime. No matter where we go, they will track us down. They have the right to do this, so the best thing for us to do is to drop into the river and stay there until they stop looking for us."

'They did this, and remained hidden all through the night. But, after the fight began, Big Whip said, "Friend, we are the reason for these deaths today. We killed Bald Eagle to show how brave we are. We did this on a dare. We should now join our band and fight alongside them."

'Both braves stripped and, taking their weapons with them, ran towards their camp. They had to pass through the enemy's lines, yet they were not noticed until they had nearly passed through them. Then they found themselves between the two warring sides.

'Just as they nearly reached their entrenchment, they turned and faced the Rees, firing at them, while jumping about to avoid getting hit, as is the Indian custom. Bullets and arrows flew around them like hail. At last they dropped, unhurt, into the Sioux entrenchment. By these actions, the two braves saved their reputations for bravery. No one in the tribe ever openly criticized them for their actions on the previous day. Young men often carry out rash actions. However, they should not be criticized for an act of bravery or else they might become cowards.

'Many were killed in the battle, but more of the Rees than of our band. About mid-afternoon, a cold fall rain began, wetting the bow strings and the flints of the guns. It looked as if the fight might have to be carried on with knives.

'But the Rees were much dispirited. They had lost many of their warriors. As their women carried off the wounded, the Blackfoot Sioux watched from the bluffs. They turned and fled towards the river. The Sioux then followed like crazy wolves, using their tomahawks to kill the tired and the slow ones. Many were killed in their boats on the river and some of the boats were shot through and sank. That was the greatest battle ever fought by our band.' The old man concluded, with a deep sigh of both satisfaction and regret.

THE THREE TESTS

Sioux

THERE DWELT IN A CERTAIN VILLAGE a woman of remarkable grace and attractiveness. The fame of her beauty drew suitors from far and near, eager to display their prowess and win the love of this imperious creature – for, besides being beautiful, she was extremely hard to please, and set such tests for her lovers as none had ever been able to satisfy.

A certain young man who lived at a considerable distance had heard of her great charms, and made up his mind to woo and win her. The difficulty of the task did not daunt him and, full of hope, he set out on his mission.

As he travelled he came to a very high hill, and on the summit he saw a man rising and sitting down at short intervals. When the prospective suitor drew nearer he observed that the man was fastening large stones to his ankles. The youth approached him, saying, 'Why do you tie there great stones to your ankles?'

'Oh,' replied the other, 'I wish to chase buffaloes, and yet whenever I do so I go beyond them, so I am tying stones to my ankles that I may not run so fast.'

'My friend,' said the suitor, 'you can run some other time. In the meantime I am without a companion; come with me.'

The Swift One agreed, and they walked on their way together. Ere they had gone very far they saw two large lakes. By the side of one of them sat a man who frequently bowed his head to the water and drank. Surprised that his thirst was not quenched, they said to him, 'Why do you sit there drinking of the lake?'

'I can never get enough water. When I have finished this lake I shall start on the other.'

'My friend,' said the suitor, 'do not trouble to drink it just now. Come and join us.'

Source
Lewis Spence,
North American Indians,
London: George
G. Harrap & Co.,
1914,
pp. 275–8

The Thirsty One complied, and the three comrades journeyed on. When they had gone a little farther they noticed a man walking along with his face lifted to the sky. Curious to know why he acted thus, they addressed him.

'Why do you walk with your eyes turned skyward?' said they.

'I have shot an arrow,' he said, 'and I am waiting for it to reappear.'

'Never mind your arrow,' said the suitor. 'Come with us.'

'I will come,' said the Skilful Archer.

As the four companions journeyed through a forest they beheld a strange sight. A man was lying with his ear to the ground, and if he lifted his head for a moment he bowed it again, listening intently. The four approached him, saying, 'Friend, for what do you listen so earnestly?'

'I am listening,' said he, 'to the plants growing. This forest is full of plants, and I am listening to their breathing.'

'You can listen when the occasion arises,' they told him. 'Come and join us.'

He agreed, and so they travelled to the village where dwelt the beautiful maiden.

When they had reached their destination they were quickly surrounded by the villagers, who displayed no small curiosity as to who their visitors were and what object they had in coming so far. When they heard that one of the strangers desired to marry the village beauty they shook their heads over him. Did he not know the difficulties in the way? Finding that he would not be turned from his purpose, they led him to a huge rock which overshadowed the village, and described the first test he would be required to meet.

'If you wish to win the maiden,' they said, 'you must first of all push away that great stone. It is keeping the sunlight from us.'

'Alas!' said the youth, 'It is impossible.'

'Not so,' said his companion of the swift foot, 'nothing could be more easy.'

Saying this, he leaned his shoulder against the rock, and with a mighty crash it fell from its place. From the breaking up of it came the rocks and stones that are scattered over all the world.

The second test was of a different nature. The people brought the strangers a large quantity of food and water, and bade them eat and drink. Being very hungry, they succeeded in disposing of the food, but the suitor sorrowfully regarded the great kettles of water.

'Alas!' said he, 'Who can drink up that?'

'I can,' said the Thirsty One, and in a twinkling he had drunk it all.

The people were amazed at the prowess of the visitors. However, they said, 'There is still another test,' and they brought out a woman who was a very swift runner, so swift that no one had ever outstripped her in a race.

'You must run a race with this woman,' said they. 'If you win you shall have the hand of the maiden you have come to seek.'

Naturally the suitor chose the Swift One for this test. When the runners were started the people hailed them as fairly matched, for they raced together till they were out of sight.

When they reached the turning point the woman said, 'Come, let us rest for a little.'

The man agreed, but no sooner had he sat down than he fell asleep. The woman seized her opportunity. Making sure that her rival was sleeping soundly, she set off for the village, running as hard as she could.

'If you wish to win the maiden, you must first of all push away that great stone.'

Meanwhile, the four comrades were anxiously awaiting the return of the competitors, and great was their disappointment when the woman came in sight, while there was yet no sign of their champion.

The man who could hear the plants growing bent his ear to the ground.

'He is asleep,' said he, 'I can hear him snoring.'

The Skilful Archer came forward, and as he bit the point off an arrow he said, 'I will soon wake him.'

He shot an arrow from the bowstring with such a wonderful aim that it wounded the sleeper's nose, and roused him from his slumbers. The runner started to his feet and looked round for the woman. She was gone. Knowing that he had been tricked, the Swift One put all his energy into an effort to overtake her. She was within a few yards of the winning post when he passed her. It was a narrow margin, but nevertheless the Swift One had gained the race for his comrade.

The youth was then married to the damsel, whom he found to be all that her admirers had claimed, and more.

THE SNAKE OGRE

Sioux

ONE DAY A YOUNG BRAVE, feeling at variance with the world in general, and wishing to rid himself of the mood, left the lodges of his people and journeyed into the forest. By and by he came to an open space, in the centre of which was a high hill. Thinking he would climb to the top and reconnoitre, he directed his footsteps thither, and as he went he observed a man coming in the opposite direction and making for the same spot. The two met on the summit, and stood for a few moments silently regarding each other. The stranger was the first to speak, gravely inviting the young brave to accompany him to his lodge and to sup with him. The other accepted the invitation, and they proceeded in the direction the stranger indicated.

On approaching the lodge the youth saw with some surprise that there was a large heap of bones in front of the door. Within sat a very old woman tending a pot. When the young man learned that the feast was to be a cannibal one, however, he declined to partake of it. The woman then boiled some corn for him, and while doing so told him that his host was nothing more nor less than a Snake Man, a sort of ogre who killed and ate human beings. Because the brave was young and very handsome the old woman took pity on him, bemoaning the fate that would surely befall him unless he could escape from the wiles of the Snake Man.

'Listen,' said she, 'I will tell you what to do. Here are some moccasins. When the morning comes put them on your feet, take one step, and you will find yourself on that headland you see in the distance. Give this paper to the man you will meet there, and he will direct you farther. But remember that however far you may go, in the evening the Snake will overtake you. When you have finished with the moccasins take them off, place them on the ground facing this way, and they will return.'

'Is that all?' said the youth.

'No,' she replied. 'Before you go you must kill me and put a robe over my bones.'

Source
Lewis Spence,
*Myths of the
American Indians,*
London: George
G. Harrap & Co.,
1914,
pp. 278–82

The young brave forthwith proceeded to carry these instructions into effect. First of all, he killed the old woman, and disposed of her remains in accordance with her bidding.

In the morning, he put on the magic moccasins which she had provided for him, and with one great step he reached the distant headland. Here he met an old man, who received the paper from him, and then, giving him another pair of moccasins, directed him to a far-off point where he was to deliver another piece of paper to a man who would await him there. Turning the first moccasins homeward, the young brave put the second pair to use, and took another gigantic step. Arrived at the second stage of his journey from the Snake's lodge, he found it a repetition of the first. He was directed to another distant spot, and from that to yet another. But when he delivered his message for the fourth time he was treated somewhat differently.

'Down there in the hollow,' said the recipient of the paper, 'there is a stream. Go towards it, and walk straight on, but do not look at the water.'

The youth did as he was bidden, and shortly found himself on the opposite bank of the stream. He journeyed up the creek, and as evening fell he came upon a place where the river widened to a lake. Skirting its shores, he suddenly found himself face to face with the Snake. Only then did he remember the words of the old woman, who had warned him that in the evening the Snake would overtake him. So he turned himself into a little fish with red fins, lazily moving in the lake.

The Snake, high on the bank, saw the little creature, and cried, 'Little Fish! Have you seen the person I am looking for? If a bird had flown over the lake you must have seen it, the water is so still, and surely you have seen the man I am seeking?'

'Not so,' replied the little fish. 'I have seen no one. But if he passes this way, I will tell you.'

So the Snake continued downstream, and as he went there was little grey Toad right in his path.

'Little Toad,' said he. 'Have you seen him for whom I am seeking? Even if only a shadow were here you must have seen it.'

'Yes,' said the little toad, 'I have seen him, but I cannot tell you which way he has gone.'

The Snake doubled and came back on his trail. Seeing a very large fish in shallow water, he said, 'Have you seen the man I am looking for?'

'That is he with whom you have just been talking,' said the fish, and the Snake turned homeward. Meeting a muskrat, he stopped.

'Have you seen the person I am looking for?' he said. Then, having his suspicions aroused, he added craftily, 'I think that you are he.'

But the muskrat began a bitter complaint.

'Just now,' said he, 'the person you seek passed over my lodge and broke it.'

So the Snake passed on and encountered a red-breasted Turtle. He repeated his query, and the turtle told him that the object of his search was to be met with farther on.

'But beware,' he added, 'for it you do not recognize him, he will kill you.'

Following the stream, the Snake came upon a large green frog floating in shallow water.

'I have been seeking a person since morning,' he said. 'I think that you are he.'

The frog allayed his suspicions, saying, 'You will meet him farther down the stream.'

The Snake next found a large turtle floating among the green scum on a lake. Getting on the turtle's back, he said, 'You must be the person I seek,' and his head rose higher and higher as he prepared to strike.

'I am not,' replied the turtle. 'The next person you meet will be he. But beware, for if you do not recognize him he will kill you.'

When he had gone a little farther down the Snake attempted to cross the stream. In the middle was an eddy. Crafty as he was, the Snake failed to recognize his enemy, and the eddy drew him down into the water and drowned him. So the youth succeeded in slaying the Snake who had sought throughout the day to kill him.

CREATION TALE
Cheyenne

THE CREATION STORY of the Cheyennes tells of a being who was floating on the surface of the water. Water-birds – swans, geese, ducks and other birds that swim – already existed, and these were all about him. The person called to these birds and asked them to bring him some earth. They were glad to do so, and agreed one after another to dive down through the water and see if they could find earth at the bottom. The larger birds dived in vain. They came up without anything, for they could not reach the bottom, but at last one small duck came to the surface with a little mud in its bill. The bird swam to the being and put the mud in his hand, and he took it and worked it with his fingers until it was dry, when he placed it in little piles on the surface of the water, and each little pile became land, and grew and grew and spread, until, as far as one could see, solid land was everywhere. Thus was created the earth we walk on.

After there was firm ground the Creator took from his right side a rib and from it made a man. From the man's left side he took a rib and from that made a woman. These two persons were made at the same place, but after they had been made they were separated by the Creator, and the woman was put far in the north, and the man in the south.

The Creator said to them, 'In that direction –' pointing to the south – 'you will find many sorts of animals and birds different from those which you will find in that direction –' pointing to the north, where the woman stood. 'The birds that live in the south will go to the north in summer. Where the woman is it will be cold and the grass and trees will not grow well. There will be hardly any of them, but where the man is everything will grow: trees, bushes, grass.'

The woman in the north, though she was grey-haired, was not old. She never seemed to grow any older. The man in the south was young. He never seemed to grow any older.

In the north lives Ho-im'-a-ha, the Winter Man, the power that brings cold and snow, and also brings sickness and death. He obeys the woman in the north. He is often spoken of in the stories and is said to have declared at a meeting of the super-natural beings that he would 'take pity on no one'. When at this meeting he spoke

The Creator made man and woman at the same place, but then they were separated, and the woman was put far in the north, and the man in the south.

Source
George Bird Grinnell, *By Cheyenne Campfires*, New Haven, Conn.: Yale University Press, 1926, pp. 16–18

in this way, the Thunder, who represents the power of the south, declared that it would not do to let Ho-im'-a-ha have everything to say; so, with the help of the buffalo, the Thunder made fire and taught one of the culture heroes how to do the same thing.

He said to Sweet Medicine, 'Get a stick and I will teach you something by which your people can warm themselves, can cook food and with which they can burn things.' He showed Sweet Medicine how to rest the point of the stick in the middle of a dried buffalo chip, and then to rub it between his hands and twirl it fast. The young man did so, and after a time the chip caught fire. Thus, by the help of the Thunder the people were given something to use against the cold, something that would warm them.

The man and woman in the south and in the north appear to typify summer and winter, the man representing the sun or the Thunder, while the woman represents the power that wars against the sun.

Twice a year there is a conflict between the Thunder and the Winter Man. At the end of summer when the streams get low and the grass becomes yellow and dry, Ho-im'-a-ha comes down from the north and says to the Thunder, 'Move back, move back, to the place from which you came. I want to spread all over the earth and freeze things and cover everything with snow.' Then the Thunder moves back. Towards spring, when the days begin to grow longer, the Thunder comes back from the south and says to Ho-im'-a-ha, 'Go back, go back, to the place from which you came; I wish to warm the earth and to make the grass grow, and all things to turn green.' Then the Winter Man moves back and the Thunder comes, bringing the rain; the grass grows and all the earth is green. So there is a struggle between these two powers. They follow each other back and forth.

The two first people, the man in the south and the woman in the north, never came together, but later other people were created and from them the earth was populated.

ORIGIN OF THE MEDICINE PIPE

Blackfoot

THUNDER – YOU HAVE HEARD HIM, he is everywhere. He roars in the mountains, he shouts far out on the prairie. He strikes the high rocks, and they fall to pieces. He hits a tree, and it is broken in slivers. He strikes the people, and they die. He is bad. He does not like the towering cliff, the standing tree, or living man. He likes to strike and crush them to the ground. Yes! Yes! Of all he is most powerful; he is the one most strong. But I have not told you the worst: he sometimes steals women.

Long ago, almost in the beginning, a man and his wife were sitting in their lodge, when Thunder came and struck them. The man was not killed. At first he was as if dead, but after a while he lived again, and rising looked about him. His wife was not there.

'Oh, well,' he thought, 'she has gone to get some water or wood.'

He sat a while; but when the sun had under-disappeared, he went out and inquired about her of the people. No one had seen her. He searched throughout the

Source
George Bird Grinnell, *Blackfoot Lodge Tales: The Story of a Prairie People*, New York: Charles Scribner's Sons, 1892, pp. 113–16

camp, but did not find her. Then he knew that Thunder had stolen her, and he went out on the hills alone and mourned. When morning came, he rose and wandered far away, and he asked all the animals he met if they knew where Thunder lived. They laughed, and would not answer.

The Wolf said, 'Do you think we would seek the home of the only one we fear? He is our only danger. From all others we can run away; but from him there is no running. He strikes, and there we lie. Turn back! Go home! Do not look for the dwelling place of that dreadful one.'

But the man kept on, and travelled far away. Now he came to a lodge – a queer lodge, for it was made of stone. It was just like any other lodge, only it was made of stone. Here lived the Raven chief. The man entered.

'Welcome, my friend,' said the chief of Ravens. 'Sit down, sit down.' And food was placed before him.

Then when he had finished eating, the Raven said, 'Why have you come?'

'Thunder has stolen my wife,' replied the man. 'I seek his dwelling place that I may find her.'

'Would you dare enter the lodge of that dreadful person?' asked the Raven. 'He lives close by here. His lodge is of stone, like this, and hanging there, within, are eyes – the eyes of those he has killed or stolen. He has taken out their eyes and hung them in his lodge. Now, then, dare you enter there?'

'No,' replied the man. 'I am afraid. What man could look at such dreadful things and live?'

'No person can,' said the Raven. 'There is but one old Thunder fears. There is but one he cannot kill. It is I, it is the Ravens. Now I will give you medicine, and he shall not harm you. You shall enter there, and seek among those eyes your wife's, and if you find them, tell that Thunder why you came, and make him give them to you. Here, now, is a raven's wing. Just point it at him, and he will start back quick. But if that fail, take this. It is an arrow, and the shaft is made of elk-horn. Take this, I say, and shoot it through the lodge.'

'Why make a fool of me?' the poor man asked. 'My heart is sad. I am crying.' And he covered his head with his robe and wept.

'Oh,' said the Raven, 'you do not believe me. Come out, come out, and I will make you believe.' When they stood outside, the Raven asked, 'Is the home of your people far?'

'A great distance,' said the man

'Can you tell how many days you have travelled?'

'No,' he replied, 'my heart is sad. I did not count the days. The berries have grown and ripened since I left.'

'Can you see your camp from here?' asked the Raven.

The man did not speak. Then the Raven rubbed some medicine on his eyes and said, 'Look!' The man looked, and saw the camp. It was close. He saw the people. He saw the smoke rising from the lodges.

'Now you will believe,' said the Raven. 'Take now the arrow and the wing, and go and get your wife.'

So the man took these things, and went to the Thunder's lodge. He entered and sat down by the doorway. The Thunder sat within and looked at him with awful eyes. But the man looked above, and saw those many pairs of eyes. Among them were those of his wife.

'Why have you come?' said the Thunder in a fearful voice.

'I seek my wife,' the man replied, 'whom you have stolen. There hang her eyes.'

'No man can enter my lodge and live,' said the Thunder, and he rose to strike him. Then the man pointed the raven wing at the Thunder, and he fell back on his couch and shivered. But he soon recovered and rose again. Then the man fitted the elk-horn arrow to his bow, and shot it through the lodge of rock. Right through the lodge of rock it pierced a jagged hole, and let the sunlight in.

'Hold,' said the Thunder. 'Stop, you are the stronger. Yours is the great medicine. You shall have your wife. Take down her eyes.' Then the man cut the string that held them, and immediately his wife stood beside him.

'Now,' said the Thunder, 'you know me. I am of great power. I live here in summer, but when winter comes, I go far south. I go south with the birds. Here is my pipe. It is medicine. Take it and keep it. Now, when I first come in the spring, you shall fill and light this pipe, and you shall pray to me, you and the people, for I bring the rain which makes the berries large and ripe. I bring the rain which makes all things grow, and for this you shall pray to me, you and all the people.'

Thus the people got the first medicine pipe. It was long ago.

'When I first come in the spring, fill and light this pipe,' said the Thunder, 'for I bring the rain which makes all things grow.'

THE FAST RUNNERS

Pawnee

ONCE, LONG AGO, the antelope and the deer met on the prairie. At this time both of them had galls and both dew claws. They began to talk together, and each was telling the other what he could do. Each one told how fast he could run, and before long they were disputing as to which could run the faster. Neither would allow that the other could beat him, so they agreed that they would have a race to decide which was the swifter, and they bet their galls on the race. When they ran, the antelope proved the faster runner, and beat the deer and took his gall.

Then the deer said, 'Yes, you have beaten me on the prairie, but that is not where I live. I only go out there sometimes to feed, or when I am travelling around. We ought to have another race in the timber. That is my home, and there I can run faster than you can.'

The antelope felt very big because he had beaten the deer in the race, and he thought wherever they might be, he could run faster than the deer. So he agreed to race in the timber, and on this race they bet their dew claws.

They ran through the thick timber, among the brush and over fallen logs, and this time the antelope ran slowly, because he was not used to this kind of travelling, and the deer easily beat him, and took his dew claws.

Since then the deer has had no gall, and the antelope no dew claws.

Source
George Bird Grinnell, *Blackfoot Lodge Tales: The Story of a Prairie People*, New York: Charles Scribner's Sons, 1892, p. 81

THE WOLF MAN

Blackfoot

THERE WAS ONCE A MAN who had two bad wives. They had no shame. The man thought if he moved away where there were no other people, he might teach these women to become good, so he moved his lodge away off on the prairie. Near where they camped was a high butte, and every evening about sundown, the man would go up on top of it, and look all over the country to see where the buffalo were feeding, and if any enemies were approaching. There was a buffalo skull on the hill, which he used to sit on.

'This is very lonesome,' said one woman to the other, one day. 'We have no one to talk with nor to visit.'

'Let us kill our husband,' said the other. 'Then we will go back to our relations and have a good time.'

Early in the morning, the man went out to hunt, and as soon as he was out of sight, his wives went up on top of the butte. There they dug a deep pit, and covered it over with light sticks, grass and dirt, and placed the buffalo skull on top.

In the afternoon they saw their husband coming home, loaded down with meat he had killed. So they hurried to cook for him. After eating, he went upon the butte and sat down on the skull. The slender sticks gave way, and he fell into the pit. His wives were watching him, and when they saw him disappear, they took down the lodge, packed everything on the dog travois, and moved off, going towards the main camp. When they got near it, so that the people could hear them, they began to cry and mourn.

'Why is this?' they were asked. 'Why are you mourning? Where is your husband?'

'He is dead,' they replied. 'Five days ago he went out to hunt, and he never came back.' And they cried and mourned again.

◆

When the man fell into the pit, he was hurt. After a while he tried to get out, but he was so badly bruised he could not climb up. A wolf, travelling along, came to the pit and saw him, and pitied him.

'Ah-h-w-o-o-o-o! Ah-h-w-o-o-o-o!' he howled, and when the other wolves heard him they all came running to see what was the matter. There came also many coyotes, badgers and kit-foxes.

'In this hole,' said the wolf, 'is my find. Here is a fallen-in man. Let us dig him out, and we will have him for our brother.'

They all thought the wolf spoke well, and began to dig. In a little while they had a hole close to the man. Then the wolf who found him said, 'Hold on, I want to speak a few words to you.'

All the animals listening, he continued, 'We will all have this man for our brother, but I found him, so I think he ought to live with us big wolves.'

All the others agreed, so the wolf went into the hole and, tearing down the rest of the dirt, dragged the almost dead man out. They gave him a kidney to eat, and when he was able to walk a little, the big wolves took him to their home. Here there was a very old blind wolf, who had powerful medicine. He cured the man,

Source
George Bird Grinnell, *Blackfoot Lodge Tales: The Story of a Prairie People*, New York: Charles Scribner's Sons, 1892, pp. 78–80

and made his head and hands look like those of a wolf. The rest of his body was not changed.

In those days the people used to make holes in the pis'kun walls (built from the foot of a cliff or canyon) and set snares, and when wolves and other animals came to steal meat, they were caught by the neck. One night the wolves all went down to the pis'kun to steal meat, and when they got close to it, the man-wolf said, 'Stand here a little while. I will go down and fix the places, so you will not be caught.'

He went on and sprang all the snares. Then he went back and called the wolves and others – the coyotes, badgers and foxes – and they all went in the pis'kun and feasted, and took meat to carry home.

In the morning the people were surprised to find the meat gone, and their nooses all drawn out. They wondered how it could have been done. For many nights the nooses were drawn and the meat stolen. But once, when the wolves went there to steal, they found only the meat of a scabby bull, and the man-wolf was angry, and cried out, 'Bad-you-give-us-o-o-o! Bad-you-give-us-o-o-o-o!'

The people heard him, and said, 'It is a man-wolf who has done all this. We will catch him.' So they put pemmican and nice back fat in the pis'kun, and many hid close by. After dark the wolves came again, and when the man-wolf saw the good food, he ran to it and began eating. Then the people all rushed in and caught him with ropes and took him to a lodge. When they got inside to the light of the fire, they knew at once who it was. They said, 'This is the man who was lost.'

'No,' said the man, 'I was not lost. My wives tried to kill me. They dug a deep hole, and I fell into it, and I was hurt so badly that I could not get out. But the wolves took pity on me and helped me, or I would have died there.'

When the people heard this, they were angry, and they told the man to do something.

'You say well,' he replied. 'I give those women to the I-kun-uh'-kah-tsi (warrior society who punished crimes against the tribe). They know what to do.'

After that night the two women were never seen again.

THE SACRED BUNDLE

Pawnee

A CERTAIN YOUNG MAN was very vain of his personal appearance, and always wore the finest clothes and richest adornments he could procure. Among other possessions he had a down feather of an eagle, which he wore on his head when he went to war, and which possessed magical properties. He was unmarried, and cared nothing for women, though doubtless there was more than one maiden of the village who would not have disdained the hand of the young hunter, for he was as brave and good-natured as he was handsome.

One day while he was out hunting with his companions – the Indians hunted on foot in those days – he got separated from the others, and followed some buffaloes for a considerable distance. The animals managed to escape, with the exception of a young cow, which had become stranded in a mud-hole. The youth fitted

Source: Lewis Spence, *North American Indians,* London: George G. Harrap & Co., 1914, pp. 304–8

an arrow to his bow, and was about to fire, when he saw that the buffalo had van-ished and only a young and pretty woman were in sight. The hunter was rather perplexed, for he could not understand where the animal had gone to, nor where the woman had come from. However, he talked to the maiden, and found her so agreeable that he proposed to marry her and return with her to his tribe. She con-sented to marry him, but only on condition that they remained where they were. To this he agreed, and gave her as a wedding gift a string of blue and white beads he wore round his neck.

One evening when he returned home after a day's hunting he found that his camp was gone and that all round about were the marks of many hoofs. No trace of his wife's body could he discover, and at last, mourning her bitterly, he returned to his tribe.

Years elapsed, and one summer morning as he was playing the stick game with his friends a little boy came towards him, wearing round his neck a string of blue and white beads.

'Father,' he said, 'mother wants you.'

The hunter was annoyed at the interruption.

'I am not your father,' he replied. 'Go away.'

The boy went away, and the man's companions laughed at him when they heard him addressed as 'father', for they knew that he was a woman-hater and that he was unmarried.

However, the boy returned in a little while. He was sent away again by the angry hunter, but one of the players now suggested that he should accompany the child and see what he wanted. All the time the hunter had been wondering where he had seen the beads before. As he reflected he saw a buffalo cow and calf run-ning across the prairie, and suddenly he remembered.

Taking his bow and arrows, he followed the buffaloes, whom he now recog-nized as his wife and child. A long and wearisome journey they had. The woman was angry with her husband, and dried up every creek they came to, so that he feared he would die of thirst, but the strategy of his son obtained food and drink for him until they arrived at the home of the buffaloes. The big bulls, the leaders of the herd, were very angry, and threatened to kill him. First, however, they gave him a test, telling him that if he accomplished it he should live. Six cows, all exact-ly alike, were placed in a row, and he was told that if he could point out his wife his life would be spared. His son helped him secretly, and he succeeded. The old bulls were surprised, and much annoyed, for they had not expected him to dis-tinguish his wife from the other cows. They gave him another test. He was requested to pick out his son from among several calves. Again the young buffalo helped him to perform the feat. Not yet satisfied, they decreed that he must run a race. If he should win they would let him go. They chose their fastest runners, but on the day set for the race a thin coating of ice covered the ground, and the buf-faloes could not run at all, while the young Indian ran swiftly and steadily, and won with ease.

The chief bulls were still angry, however, and determined that they would kill him, even though he had passed their tests. So they made him sit on the ground, all the strongest and fiercest bulls round him. Together they rushed at him, and in a little while his feather was seen floating in the air. The chief bulls called on the others to stop, for they were sure that he must be trampled to pieces by this time.

The strongest and fiercest bulls rushed at the indian, but when they drew back there he sat in the centre of the circle with his feather in his hair.

But when they drew back there sat the Indian in the centre of the circle, with his feather in his hair.

It was, in fact, his magic feather to which he owed his escape, and a second rush which the buffaloes made had as little effect on him. Seeing that he was possessed of magical powers, the buffaloes made the best of matters and welcomed him into their camp, on condition that he would bring them gifts from his tribe. This he agreed to do.

When the Indian returned with his wife and son to the village people, they found that there was no food to be had. But the buffalo-wife produced some meat from under her robe, and they ate of it. Afterwards they went back to the herd with gifts, which pleased the buffaloes greatly. The chief bulls, knowing that the people were in want of food, offered to return with the hunter. His son, who also wished to return, arranged to accompany the herd in the form of a buffalo, while his parents went ahead in human shape. The father warned the people that they must not kill his son when they went to hunt buffaloes, for, he said, the yellow calf would always return leading more buffaloes.

By and by the child came to his father saying that he would no more visit the camp in the form of a boy, as he was about to lead the herd eastward. Ere he went he told his father than when the hunters sought the chase they should kill the yellow calf and sacrifice it to Atius Tirawa, tan its hide, and wrap in the skin an ear of corn and other sacred things. Every year they should look out for another yellow calf, sacrifice it and keep a piece of its fat to add to the bundle. Then when food was scarce and famine threatened the tribe, the chiefs should gather in council and pay a friendly visit to the young buffalo, and he would tell Tirawa of their need, so that another yellow calf might be sent to lead the herd to the people.

When he had said this the boy left the camp. All was done as he had ordered. Food became plentiful, and the father became a chief, greatly respected by his people. His buffalo-wife, however, he almost forgot, and one night she vanished. So distressed was the chief, and so remorseful for his neglect of her, that he never recovered, but withered away and died. But the sacred bundle was long preserved in the tribe as a magic charm to bring the buffalo.

THE ADVENTURES OF ICTINIKE

Iowa

MANY TALES ARE TOLD by the Iowa Indians regarding Ictinike, the son of the sun god, who had offended his father, and was consequently expelled from the celestial regions. He possessed a very bad reputation among the Indians for deceit and trickery. They say that he taught them all the evil things they know, and they seem to regard him as a Father of Lies.

Source
Lewis Spence,
North American Indians,
London: George
G. Harrap &
Co., 1914,
pp. 266–71

I

One day Ictinike encountered the Rabbit, and hailed him in a friendly manner, calling him 'grandchild', and requesting him to do him a service. The Rabbit expressed his willingness to assist the god to the best of his ability, and inquired what he wished him to do.

'Oh, grandchild,' said the crafty one, pointing upwards to where a bird circled in the blue vault above them, 'take your bow and arrow and bring down yonder bird.'

The Rabbit fitted an arrow to his bow, and the shaft transfixed the bird, which fell like a stone and lodged in the branches of a great tree.

'Now, grandchild,' said Ictinike, 'go into the tree and fetch me the game.'

This, however, the Rabbit at first refused to do, but at length he took off his clothes and climbed into the tree, where he stuck fast among the tortuous branches.

Ictinike, seeing that he could not make his way down, donned the unfortunate Rabbit's garments, and, highly amused at the animal's predicament, betook himself to the nearest village. There he encountered a chief who had two beautiful daughters, the elder of whom he married. The younger daughter, regarding this as an affront to her personal attractions, wandered off into the forest in a fit of the sulks.

As she paced angrily up and down she heard someone calling to her from above, and, looking upwards, she beheld the unfortunate Rabbit, whose fur was adhering to the natural gum that exuded from the bark of the tree. The girl cut down the tree and lit a fire near it, which melted the gum and freed the Rabbit. The Rabbit and the chief's daughter, after discussing things, discovered that the being who had tricked the one and affronted the other was the same. Together they proceeded to the chief's lodge, where the girl was laughed at because of the strange companion she had brought back with her.

Suddenly an eagle appeared in the air above them. Ictinike shot at and missed it, but the Rabbit loosed an arrow with great force and brought it to earth. Each morning a feather of the bird became another eagle, and each morning Ictinike shot at and missed this newly created bird, which the Rabbit invariably succeeded in killing. This went on until Ictinike had quite worn out the Rabbit's clothing and was wearing a very old piece of tent skin; but the Rabbit returned to him the garments he had been forced to don when Ictinike had stolen his. Then the Rabbit commanded the Indians to beat the drums, and each time they were beaten Ictinike jumped so high that every bone in his body was shaken. At length, after a more than usually loud series of beats, he leapt to such a height that when he came down it was found that the fall had broken his neck. The Rabbit was avenged.

II

One day Ictinike, footsore and weary, encountered a buzzard, which he asked to oblige him by carrying him on its back part of the way. The crafty bird immediately consented, and, seating Ictinike between its wings, flew off with him.

They had not gone far when they passed above a hollow tree, and Ictinike began to shift uneasily in his seat as he observed the buzzard hovering over it. He requested the bird to fly onward, but for answer it cast him headlong into the tree trunk, where he found himself a prisoner. For a long time he lay there in want and wretchedness, until at last a large hunting party struck camp at the spot. Ictinike chanced to be wearing some racoon skins, and he thrust the tails of these through the cracks in the tree. Three women who were standing near imagined that a number of racoons had become imprisoned in the hollow trunk, and they made a large hole in it for the purpose of capturing them. Ictinike at once emerged, whereupon the women fled. Ictinike lay on the ground pretending to be dead, and as he was covered with the racoon skins the birds of prey, the eagle, the rook and the magpie, came to devour him. While they pecked at him the buzzard made his appearance for the purpose of joining in the feast, but Ictinike, rising quickly, tore the feathers from its scalp. That is why the buzzard has no feathers on its head.

THE GHOST BRIDE

Pawnee

IN A PLACE WHERE WE USED to have a village, a young woman died just before the tribe started on the hunt. When she died they dressed her up in her finest clothes and buried her, and soon after this the tribe started on the hunt.

A party of young men had gone off to visit another tribe, and they did not get back until after this girl had died and the tribe had left the village. Most of this party did not go back to the village, but met the tribe and went with them on the hunt. Among the young men who had been away was one who had loved this girl who had died. He went back alone to the village. It was empty and silent, but before he reached it, he could see, far off, someone sitting on top of a lodge. When he came near, he saw that it was the girl he loved. He did not know that she had died, and he wondered to see her there alone, for the time was coming when he would be her husband and she his wife. When she saw him coming, she came down from the top of the lodge and went inside. When he came close to her, he spoke and said, 'Why are you here alone in the village?'

She answered him, 'They have gone off on the hunt. I was sulky with my relations, and they went off and left me behind.'

The man wanted her now to be his wife, but the girl said to him, 'No, not yet, but later we will be married.' She said to him, 'You must not be afraid. Tonight there will be dances here; the ghosts will dance.'

This is an old custom of the Pawnees. When they danced they used to go from one lodge to another, singing, dancing and hallooing. So now, then the tribe had gone and the village was deserted, the ghosts did this. He could hear them coming along the empty streets and going from one lodge to another. They came into the lodge where he was, and danced about, and whooped and sang, and sometimes they almost touched him, and he came pretty near being scared.

The next day, the young man persuaded the girl to go on with him and follow the tribe, to join it on the hunt. They started to travel together, and she promised him that she would surely be his wife, but not until the time came. They overtook the tribe; but before they got to the camp, the girl stopped.

She said, 'Now we have arrived, but you must go first to the village, and prepare a place for me. Where I sleep, let it be behind a curtain. For four days and four nights I must remain behind this curtain. Do not speak of me. Do not mention my name to anyone.'

The young man left her there and went into the camp. When he got to his lodge, he told a woman, one of his relations, to go out to a certain place and bring in a woman who was waiting there for him.

His relative asked him, 'Who is the woman?'

The ghosts came into the lodge where the man was, and danced about and whooped and sang.

Source
George Bird Grinnell, *Pawnee Hero Stories and Folk-Tales*, New York: Forest and Stream Publishing Company, 1889, pp. 143–6

And to avoid speaking her name, he told who were her father and mother.

His relation, in surprise, said, 'It cannot be that girl, for she died some days before we started on the hunt.'

When the woman went to look for the girl she could not find her. The girl had disappeared. The young man had disobeyed her, and had told who she was. She had told him that she must stay behind a curtain for four days, and that no one must know who she was. Instead of doing what she had said, he told who she was, and the girl disappeared because she was a ghost. If he had obeyed the girl, she would have lived a second time upon earth. That same night this young man died in sleep.

Then the people were convinced that there must be a life after this one.

OLD MAN AND THE LYNX

Blackfoot

OLD MAN WAS TRAVELLING round over the prairie when he saw a lot of prairie dogs sitting in a circle. They had built a fire and were sitting around it. Old Man went towards them, and when he got near them, he began to cry and said, 'Let me, too, sit by that fire.' The prairie dogs said, 'All right, Old Man. Don't cry. Come and sit by the fire.' Old Man sat down, and saw that the prairie dogs were playing a game. They would put one of their number in the fire and cover him up with the hot ashes; and then, after he had been there a little while, he would say *sk, sk,* and they would push the ashes off him and pull him out.

Old Man said, 'Teach me how to do that'; and they told him what to do, and put him in the fire, and covered him up with the ashes, and after a little while he said *sk, sk,* like a prairie dog, and they pulled him out again. Then he did it to the prairie dogs. At first he put them in one at a time, but there were many of them, and pretty soon he got tired and said, 'Come, I will put you all in at once.' They said, 'Very well, Old Man,' and all got in the ashes; but just as Old Man was about to cover them up, one of them, a female heavy with young, said, 'Do not cover me up; the heat may hurt my children, which are about to be born.' Old Man said, 'Very well. If you do not want to be covered up, you can sit over by the fire and watch the rest.' Then he covered up all the others.

At length the prairie dogs said *sk, sk,* but Old Man did not sweep the ashes off and pull them out of the fire. He let them stay there and die. The old she one ran off to a hole and, as she went down in it, said *sk, sk.* Old Man chased her, but he got to the hole too late to catch her. So he said, 'Oh, well, you can go. There will be more prairie dogs by and by.'

When the prairie dogs were roasted, Old Man cut a lot of red willow brush to lay them on, and then sat down and began to eat. He ate until he was full, and then felt sleepy. He said to his nose, 'I am going to sleep now. Watch for me and wake me up in case anything comes near.' Then the Old Man slept. Pretty soon his nose snored, and he woke up and said, 'What is it?' The nose said, 'A raven is flying over there.' Old Man said, 'That is nothing,' and went to sleep again. Soon his nose snored again. Old Man said, 'What is it now?' The nose said, 'There is a coyote over there, coming this way.' Old Man said, 'A coyote is nothing,' and again went to

Source
George Bird Grinnell, *Blackfoot Lodge Tales: The Story of a Prairie People,* New York: Charles Scribner's Sons, 1892, pp. 171–3

sleep. Presently his nose snored again, but Old Man did not wake up. Again it snored, and called out, 'Wake up, a bob cat is coming.' Old Man paid no attention. He slept on.

The bob cat crept up to where the fire was and ate up all the roast prairie dogs, and then went off and lay down on a flat rock, and went to sleep. All this time the nose kept trying to wake Old Man up, and at last he awoke, and the nose said, 'A bob cat is over there on that flat rock. He has eaten all your food.' Then Old Man called out loud, he was so angry. He went softly over to where the bob cat lay and seized it, before it could wake up to bite or scratch him. The bob cat cried out, 'Hold on, let me speak a word or two.' But Old Man would not listen; he said, 'I will teach you to steal my food.' He pulled off the lynx's tail, pounded his head against the rock so as to make his face flat, pulled him out long, so as to make him small-bellied, and then threw him away into the brush. As he went sneaking off, Old Man said, 'There, that is the way you bob cats shall always be.' That is the reason the lynxes look so today.

BIBLIOGRAPHY

Alexander, Hartley Burr, *The Mythology of All Races*, New York: Cooper Square Publishers, Inc., 1964

Beach, William W., *The Indian Miscellany: Containing Papers on the History, Antiquities, Arts, Languages, Religions, Traditions, and Superstitions of the American Aborigines*, Albany: J. Munsell Publishing Co., 1877.

Burland, Cottie, *North American Indian Mythology*, London: Paul Hamlyn Limited, 1965

Burlin, Natalie Curtis, *The Indians' Book*, New York: Harper and Brothers, 1923

Bushnell, David, 'The Choctaw of Bayou Lacomb, St Tammany Parish, LA', *BAE Bulletin*, 48 (1909)
  'Myths of the Louisiana Choctaw', *American Anthropologist*, 12 (1910)

Curtin, Jeremiah, *Creation Myths of Primitive America*, New York: Benjamin Blom, 1898

De Angulo, Jaime, *Indian Tales*, New York: A.A. Wyn, Inc., 1953

Dorsey, George A, 'Traditions of the Caddo', *Carnegie Institution*, 41 (1905)

Dorsey, J.O., 'Two Biloxi Tales', *JAFL*, 6 (1893)

Driver, Harold, E., *Indians of North America*, Chicago: University of Chicago Press, 1961

Dunn, Jacob P., *True Indian Stories* (with glossary of Indiana Indian names), Indianapolis: Centinel Printing Co., 1908

Eastman, Charles A., *Old Indian Days*, New York: McClure Company, 1907

Emerson, Ellen R., *Indian Myths; or, Legends, Traditions, and Symbols of the Aborigines of America*, Boston: J.R. Osgood and Co., 1884

Fewkes, J. Walter, 'How the Medicine Man was Born, and How He Turned a Man into a Tree', *JAFL*, 3 (1884)

Fletcher, Alice C., *Indian Story and Song from North America*, Boston: Small, Maynard, and Co., 1900

Foster, J. W., *Prehistoric Races of the United States of America*, Chicago: S.C. Griggs & Co. 1874

Gatschet, Albert S., 'Some Mythic Stories of the Yuchi Indians', *American Anthropologist*, (OS) 6 (1893)

Greenlee, R.F., 'The Milky Way', *JAFL*, 58 (1945)
  'Men Visit the Sky to see God', *JAFL*, 58 (1945)

Grinnell, George Bird, *Pawnee Hero Stories and Folk-Tales*, New York: Forest and Stream Publishing Company, 1889
  Blackfoot Lodge Tales: The Story of a Prairie People, New York: Charles Scribner's Sons, 1892
  By Cheyenne Campfires, New Haven, Conn: Yale University Press, 1926

Halbert, Henry S., 'Nanih Waiya, the Sacred Mound of the Choctaws', *Publications of Mississippi Historical Society*, 2 (1899)

Hale, Horatio, *Iroquois Book of Rites*, Philadelphia: D.G. Brinton, 1883

Hultkrantz, Ake, *Native Religions of North America: The Power of Visions and Fertility*, San Francisco: Harper & Row Publishers, 1987

Johnson, Elias, *Legends, Traditions, and Laws of the Iroquois, or Six Nations*, Lockport, NY: Union Printing and Publishing Co., 1881

Josephy Jr, Alvin M., *The Indian Heritage of America*, Boston: Houghton Mifflin Company, 1991

500 Nations: An Illustrated History of North American Indians, New York: Alfred A. Knopf, 1994

Kate, H., 'The Hero with the Horned Snake', *JAFL*, 2 (1889)

Leland, Charles, G., *The Algonquin Legends of New England*, Boston: Houghton, Mifflin, and Company, 1884

Mails, Thomas E., *Plains Indians: Dog Soldiers, Bear Men and Buffalo Women*, New York: Bonanza Books, 1973

Martin, Paul S., *et al.*, *Indians Before Columbus: Twenty Thousand Years of North American History Revealed by Archeology*, Chicago: University of Chicago Press, 1947

Mooney, James, 'Myths of the Cherokees.' *BAEAR*, 19 (1900)

'The Cherokee Play Ball'. *BAEAR*, 24 (1907)

Prince, John, 'Notes on Passamaquoddy Literature', *Annals of the New York Academy of Science*, 11 (1898) and 23 (1901)

Radin, Paul, *The Trickster: A Study in American Indian Mythology*, New York: Bell Publishing, Inc., 1956

Salomon, Julian Harris, *The Book of Indian Crafts and Lore*, New York: Harper and Brothers, 1928

Schoolcraft, Henry R., *North American Indian Legends*, Philadelphia: J.B. Lippincott & Co., 1856

Skinner, Charles, *Myths and Legends of Our Own Land*, (3 vols.), Philadelphia: J.B. Lippincott & Co., 1896; reprinted by Singing Tree Press, Michigan, 1969

Smith, E.A., *Myths of the Iroquois, BAEAR*, 2, 1881

Speck, Frank G., 'The Creek Indians of Taskigi Town', *American Anthropological Society Memoirs*, 2, 2 (1907)

'Penobscot Tales', *JAFL*, 48 (1935)

Spence, Lewis, *The Myths of the North American Indians*, London: George G. Harrap & Co., 1914

Spencer, Robert F., and Jesse D. Jennings, *The Native Americans*, New York: Harper & Row, 1965

Swanton, John R., 'Adoption of the Human Race' and 'Creation', *BAE Bulletin*, 42 (1924–5)

'The Celestial Canoe', *BAE Bulletin*, 42 (1924–5)

'How Rabbit Fooled Alligator', *BAE Bulletin*, 88 (1929)

'Myths and Tales of the Southeastern Indians', *BAE Bulletin*, 88 (1929)

'The Walnut-cracker', *BAE Bulletin*, 88 (1929)

The Indians of the Southeastern United States, Washington, DC: US Government Printing Office, 1946

Waldman, Carl, *Atlas of the North American Indian*, New York: Facts on File Publications, 1985

Wissler, Clark, *Indians of the United States*, Garden City, NY: Doubleday & Company, Inc., 1966

Wood, Charles, and Erskine Scott, *A Book of Tales: Being Some Myths of the North American Indians*, New York: Vanguard Press, 1929

INDEX